Furniture Finishing
& Refinishing

By the Editors of Sunset Books
and Sunset Magazine

Sunset Publishing Corporation ■ Menlo Park, California

Foreword

Almost any piece of wooden furniture is worth saving and we're thankful to the people who have helped us with many of the restoration projects in this book. For their time, elbow grease, and attention to detail, we'd like to thank Earle T. Stebben (refinisher), Peter Whiteley, Linda Brandt, Brian Schmidt, Louise Watson, and Alice Masterson.

For their help and generosity, our special thanks go to Jim and Bernice Furcell, Ray Loughlin, Don White Jr., June Montgomery, and all of the people who were kind enough to let us beautify their furniture.

Research and Text: Chris Payne

Supervising Editor: Jack McDowell

Design and Artwork: Ted Martine

Photography: Ells Marugg

Cover: Victorian sewing table receives a new shellac finish (directions on page 38). Photographed by Ells Marugg.

Editor, Sunset Books: Elizabeth L. Hogan

Twelfth printing November 1990

Contents

Special features

When your furniture needs a face lift

An introduction to do-it-yourself wood finishing

Few homes are without one or more furniture pieces that could be given a new lease on life by re-finishing. Then, too, the enduring respect for antiques and the continuing popularity of unfinished furniture have stimulated many people's interest in developing wood finishing skills.

A good furniture finish provides excellent protection for the open pores and grain of wood. A furniture finish also gives wood a pleasing appearance, sometimes adding lively decoration and accent.

You'll find it is easy to produce a first-rate finishing job using only basic equipment and following the common-sense finishing procedures explained in this book. Whether your interest in working on furniture is motivated by necessity, art, or the desire for a simple diversion, do-it-yourself furniture finishing is both a practical and a pleasing activity—easy on the pocketbook and soothing to the mind.

Finishing—an honored craft

Wood finishing has traditionally been one of the most respected trades in woodworking. To create a clear, durable finish on a well-built piece of furniture once required a craftsman noted for his extensive practical knowledge and fine workmanship. Furniture finishing was an honored craft.

Today, modern finishing materials and techniques have cleared up much of the mystery surrounding wood finishing. Selecting and applying a wood stain and the final protective coat are now no more difficult than any other household maintenance activity—and much more rewarding.

TRADITIONAL FINISHES & MODERN DEVELOPMENTS

The principles of finishing wood for decoration and durability have remained virtually unchanged for centuries. Recent discoveries of furniture and art objects built between 1500 and 1000 B.C. reveal multiple clear coats of fossil vegetable gum—often produced from amber—which is still the base for many of the natural-resin varnishes used today.

Shellac—resin produced from the shell-like scale of the lac bug—was first used in India in about 1600 and later became the most popular finish of 19th century Europe.

In contrast, modern lacquer, catalytic sealers, synthetic penetrating resins, and polyurethanes are all recent developments.

Chemical advances are being made at such a pace that, of all the major home improvement products on the market today, probably none change as rapidly as furniture-finishing materials.

Deciding which project you'll start on is first step in furniture finishing. Choose a piece that needs little if any repair—a piece you'll be proud to use when final finishing or refinishing is completed.

Prepare old furniture for refinishing **(far left)** by removing all non-wood accessories—upholstery, knobs, drawer handles. **Near left:** Reamalgamation is simple way to repair blushing, water marks, scratches, other defects in furniture finish. Always try this process before you begin to refinish a piece completely.

Always consult your paint dealer for the most current product information before beginning any finishing or refinishing project—it's his business to know what he sells.

IF IT'S WOOD, IT'S WORTH SAVING

Anyone who goes shopping for furniture today can get a good idea of the present value of wood. Reasonably priced furniture, when you can find it, is often a blend of plastic laminates, composition particle-board, and plywoods; the quality of construction is frequently not up to par.

If you've noticed the growing popularity of "nude" or unfinished furniture stores in your area or have purchased such furniture yourself, you probably understand why people feel more confident when they can actually "see" what they're buying.

Genuine furniture woods have a versatility, a warmth, and a beauty that only nature can create. And, since all wooden furniture is worth saving, regardless of its condition, only minimal knowledge, preparation, and patience are necessary to insure trouble-free furniture finishing results.

Decisions. decisions. decisions

Before you begin to finish or refinish furniture, you must make certain basic decisions.

Your first decision is to select the piece of furniture to work on. All your other decisions will depend on what particular work needs to be done to that piece.

Often the furniture you choose will need minor repair before it is ready for finishing. Take care of these repairs first (see pages 16-19), because once you begin applying the finish, it is difficult to go back and reglue something you have missed.

In some cases, a thorough cleaning with weak ammonia or solvent is the only work an old piece of furniture needs. Many clean but slightly worn finishes require only a clear, rejuvenating coat of varnish to bring their surface luster back to original condition.

A clear finish is not the only way to give new life to discarded furniture, though. Opaque finishes (paint, enamel, two-tone glazes) can be applied over an old finish. In fact, an opaque finish may be the only answer if the piece you are refinishing is of marginal quality or construction.

WHERE SHOULD I START?

By picking up this book. You probably have it in hand because you feel a certain piece of furniture needs a new finish.

If the furniture is new, you can skip pages 13-19—they deal mostly with refinishing. But if your piece is older, it already has a finish, so try to determine if it's worth saving before you launch into a total refinishing effort.

Furniture selection can begin right in your own home. If this is your first attempt at refinishing, don't plan to start with the scratched dining room table. Save such major projects until you have gained experience with a smaller piece—a chair, an end table, or whatever you feel you can handle.

Select only furniture that is in reasonably good shape; furniture needing major repairs should be set aside until you feel more confident about your woodworking skills. And choose furniture you will be proud to use when the job is done.

Finishing vs. refinishing decisions are easy ones. If you have just built a new piece or purchased one from an unfinished furniture store, you are interested in the first "finishing" process. (Special hints for unfinished furniture are on pages 24-25.)

But if your first project comes from a garage sale, flea market, or your grandmother's attic, you can be fairly certain that some form of finish has previously been applied.

If the old finish can't be saved or rejuvenated (see page 65), it will have to come off before regular wood "finishing" can begin.

Old patina vs. the new-wood look is one important option you should consider from the beginning. The word "patina" often confuses the beginning refinisher. Patina is a darkening of the wood surface brought on by changes in the atmosphere and by the aging process. Though common to all woods, it lends particular species (pine, for example) an especially impressive look.

Many experts feel that a piece of furniture requires about 100 years of aging to acquire an impressive patina. It is this delicate coloring that adds much to the value of an antique, distinguishing a truly lovely old piece from a modern reproduction or an outright impostor.

In place of the more natural aging process, however, colorful patinas can frequently be simulated on furniture by carefully applying stains and final protective finishes. Making wood look "old" is easy to do, especially with new, unfinished furniture, and may sometimes even be necessary if your antique's original patina has accidentally been damaged.

Of course, a cleaner, brighter, more contemporary wood look may appeal to you instead. If that is the case, remove any of the previous surface coloring that offends you and start anew with the finish of your choice.

Whichever look you choose, always take care throughout the stripping and refinishing processes to see that the age-old character of authentic antique furniture is not destroyed.

TRY TO SALVAGE AN OLD FINISH

Save yourself time and effort on any refinishing job by deciding whether or not the old finish must be totally removed. In many cases it needn't be (see New Life for an Old Finish, page 65).

Often all an old finish needs is a good cleaning followed by a quick overcoat of some clear finishing material. Any time you don't have to strip off all the old paint or varnish, you save yourself a great deal of work.

Clean off the surface before you make any refinishing decisions. Many old finishes are just dirty or need only minor repair to restore their original beauty.

There is no one best way to clean a dirty finish—it depends on the kind of dirt. Probably the safest first approach is to use a rag moistened with paint thinner (mineral spirits), which will effectively dissolve polish, wax, oil, and greasy grime.

If paint thinner doesn't work, try a solution of 20 percent household ammonia and 80 percent water. Use this cleaning solution sparingly because water can loosen many of the old glues that hold antiques together. Since the important thing is to avoid water buildup, use a rag or sponge that is just damp. Work carefully.

Analyze the old finish from the point of view of doing the least possible work to get it back into shape. If the old finish is not adhering to the wood because it is badly scratched or chipped in some places, or if the old finish is paint and you would like the wood grain to show, plan on removing the finish down to the bare wood.

Determine what the old finish is so you can have some idea of how to repair it. Test for a particular finish by applying its solvent to an out-of-the-way portion of the furniture where it won't be noticed.

Most pre-1920s clear finishes contain shellac and are dissolvable in denatured alcohol.

Nearly all commercial furniture made after 1920 has been sprayed with lacquer, which dissolves in lacquer thinner. Varnishes and paints can often be softened by lacquer thinner or commercial paint removers but must be scraped off the wood—they do not dissolve.

Try to repair the old finish before you decide on total finish removal. You really have nothing to lose. Pages 65-68 describe in detail the process of repairing old finishes, and you will realize it is fairly easy when you compare it to the job of removing the old finish and refinishing.

Many products now on the market are said to be "instant" furniture refinishers. They work on the principle of reamalgamation (see Alternatives to Refinishing, page 66), and because they often consist of a blend of alcohol, lacquer thinners, and other solvents, they are frequently quite effective.

WHAT TO LOOK FOR IN A NEW FINISH

For any piece of furniture you select, there could be at least two or three finishes that seem equally appropriate. Choosing the right finish is often a matter of weighing several factors against each other and deciding on a finish that best meets your needs.

Appearance is probably the first finishing characteristic that comes to mind. Some furniture finishes leave the wood surface perfectly smooth; others emphasize the open wood pores and grain. Some wood stains complement a certain piece of furniture; others hide the natural beauty of the wood's color and pattern.

If the piece of furniture you choose for your project is destined for your living room, don't feel that its finish must match any of the other pieces in the room. Within reasonable limits, contrasts in finish, color, or texture will add interest to all your other furnishings.

On the other hand, a room full of furniture finished in exactly the same way is likely to be boring. If you're faced with such monotony in your own home, you might be encouraged to do more refinishing than you had first intended.

Durability is one of the finishing attributes you might not have thought of. Any finish you select for your furniture is fine, as long as it pleases you. But if your newly finished furniture is subject to constant wear and abuse from children and animals, or if you do a lot of entertaining, then choose a finish you can be sure will withstand rough treatment and protect your valuable wood at the same time.

Ease of application is another aspect to consider. Some finishes are brushed onto the wood and are ready for use in a few hours; others must be applied in several coats and demand much rubbing in between coats.

Modern finishes are advertised for their ease of application and time-saving qualities. Even so, you'll find that a little extra effort on your part in applying a finish

(Continued on page 10)

Your finishing options

All furniture finishes can be divided into three basic types: clear finishes, stains, and enamels. Whenever selecting a specific finish, always read the label carefully for manufacturer's instructions. Make sure that all products you purchase are chemically compatible.

CLEAR FINISHES. These are the most popular finishes when working with quality wood. A clear finish protects and allows the beauty of wood texture, color, and grain to show through. Choose between a glossy, semigloss, or flat sheen and any one of a number of stains under the clear final coat.

STAINS. These dyes or pigments are most frequently used under other clear finishes. Because stains can effectively disguise wood grain, they are useful for transforming an inexpensive piece of furniture into one that looks old and valuable.

ENAMELS. Although paint is the most common finish for wood, most painting is done on walls, doors, or ceilings—rarely on furniture. When wood has been burned or discolored (or is of marginal natural beauty) and painting is necessary, use colorful enamels for decoration and durability.

Know your woods

The color photographs on these two pages show a selection of the most popular woods commonly used in building furniture. Since you'll want to know what type of wood you're working with before beginning any furniture finishing project, this section should prove particularly helpful.

Often true wood characteristics can be camouflaged by pigmented stains, fillers, or semiopaque final finishes. Whenever possible, try to make sure that your wood is free from these disguises before you attempt to identify it.

For identification, match the photographed wood against such details of your furniture's wood as its pores, its characteristic grain pattern, and the natural color of its surface. Then turn to pages 10-11 to learn more about this particular wood's properties, range of growth, and common uses—and the finishing methods recommended for it.

Oak   Maple   Walnut   Pine

Birch   Cherry   Ash   Mahogany

Beech

Poplar

Teak

Pecan

Elm

Rosewood

Fir

Redwood

Cedar

Sycamore

Butternut

Basswood

...Continued from page 7

will always result in a better-than-average job.

Traditional finishes often take longer to apply, but don't let that discourage you. There are still many furniture finishers around who believe that, when it comes to a beautiful wood surface, you get what you pay for, in time as well as in effort.

Ease of maintenance might possibly be the most important thing to think about when choosing a finish. Some furniture finishes require consistently more work than others—waxing, polishing, repairing scratches, and just keeping the dust and dirt off.

Regardless of what finish you choose, if it is to serve you well through the years, it will require some form of continuing maintenance. Good finishes, given proper care, should last a lifetime.

A guide to wood differences

Different furniture woods often have different properties of weight, color, strength, pore size, and grain figure. These properties are most important to the woodworker and wood finisher both when determining which wood is to be used for a specific project and when choosing which finish is to be applied to the wood when completing the project.

First refer to the photographs on pages 8-9 to help you identify the woods you'll most likely be working with. Then look for the woods' individual description on these two pages to learn something about their characteristics, specific uses, and suggested final finishes.

ASH, White (*Fraxinus americana*). *Source:* The Great Lakes states, New England, and generally the central United States. *Color and Pattern:* Grayish through creamy white to a reddish dark brown. Distinct straight grain and open pores. *Characteristics:* Tough, heavy, and hard with good shock resistance. *Uses:* Baseball bats, tool handles, watertight cooperage, furniture—especially bent wood chair parts. *Finish:* Apply clear finish over bare wood or over light or dark stain.

BASSWOOD (*Tilia americana*). *Source:* Northern United States and Canada. *Color and Pattern:* Creamy white to creamy brown with frequent reddish markings. Faint growth rings and broad wood rays which are darker than the background wood; small wood pores. *Characteristics:* Lightweight and moderately stiff; very weak with a low resistance to shock. *Uses:* Boxes and crates, millwork, and furniture. *Finish:* Apply clear finish over light or dark stain. Also consider painting with colored enamel.

BEECH, American (*Fagus grandifolia*). *Source:* Great Lake states and the Appalachian region. *Color and Pattern:* Reddish brown heartwood and creamy white sapwood. Conspicuous wood rays with tiny and virtually invisible wood pores. *Characteristics:* Hard, strong, stiff, excellent shock resistance. Also completely tasteless and odorless. *Uses:* Boxes, food containers, furniture, floors, and tool handles. *Finish:* Apply clear finish over bare wood or over stain.

BIRCH, Yellow (*Betula alleghaniensis*). *Source:* Canada, the Great Lake states and from New England to North Carolina. *Color and Pattern:* Creamy white to light reddish brown; extremely small wood pores. *Characteristics:* Heavy, hard, strong, and stiff with very good shock resistance. *Uses:* Spools, bobbins, dowels, woodenware, and furniture. Probably the best wood for imitating cherry. *Finish:* Apply clear finish over bare wood or over light or dark stain.

BUTTERNUT (*Juglans cinerea*), also called White Walnut, etc. *Source:* North central states and southern Canada. *Color and Pattern:* Pale to dark brown with occasional dark streaks running throughout. Large, open wood pores. *Characteristics:* Soft to medium texture; only moderate shock resistance. *Uses:* Interior millwork and furniture. *Finish:* Apply clear finish over bare wood or over light or dark stain.

CEDAR, Aromatic Red (*Juniperus virginiana*), also called Tennessee Red Cedar, etc. *Source:* Eastern two-thirds of the United States. Largest production in southeastern and south central states. *Color and Pattern:* Light red with light colored streaks running throughout. Knotty pattern and other natural markings are always present. *Characteristics:* Highly aromatic and moderately hard, though brittle. *Uses:* Storage chests, closet lining, lead pencils, small articles of woodenware. *Finish:* Leave unfinished or apply thin, clear finish over bare wood.

CHERRY, Black (*Prunus serotina*). *Source:* Maine west to the Dakotas and south along the Appalachians. *Color and Pattern:* Light to dark reddish brown. Straight grain and small, individual pores. *Characteristics:* Moderately hard and heavy; good shock and wear resistance. *Uses:* Furniture, woodenware, caskets, pattern making. *Finish:* Apply clear finish over bare wood. Can be lightly stained.

ELM, American (*Ulmus americana*), Rock Elm (*Ulmus thomasii*). *Source:* Eastern United States except in the Appalachian highlands, and southern Florida. *Color and Pattern:* Light brown to dark brown, often containing shades of red. Straight grain pattern with obvious light and dark boundaries. *Characteristics:* Moderately hard and heavy; good shock resistance. Excellent bending qualities. *Uses:* Boxes and crates, cooperage, furniture—especially bent wood chair parts. *Finish:* Apply clear finish over light or dark stain.

FIR, including Douglas fir (*Pseudotsuga menziesii*) and many local so-called "White" Firs. *Source:* Pacific and Rocky Mountain states. *Color and Pattern:* Creamy white to yellowish with obvious differences between spring and summer growth. *Characteristics:* Moderately heavy, hard, and stiff. Pronounced resin canals and wild grain markings make this a difficult wood to finish. *Uses:* Construction, plywood, boxes and crates, hidden parts of furniture. *Finish:* Apply clear finish over bare wood or over light or dark stain. Use sealer before staining. Also consider painting with colored enamel.

MAHOGANY, Honduras (*Swietenia macrophylla*), other types include Cuban Mahogany, African Mahogany, Philippine Mahogany (Lauan), etc. *Source:* Central America, Brazil, Peru, other tropical climates. *Color and Pattern:* Yellowish brown through reddish brown to dark red. Frequently highly figured grain pattern and open wood pores. *Characteristics:* Extremely stable, moderately hard, even textured, and heavy. *Uses:* Furniture, paneling, pattern making, and boatbuilding. *Finish:* Apply clear finish over bare wood. Can be lightly stained.

MAPLE, Hard (*Acer saccharum*), also called Bird's Eye Maple, Sugar Maple, etc. *Source:* Northwest United States, Great Lake states, Canada. *Color and Pattern:* Creamy white to light reddish brown. Frequently straight grain and tiny wood pores. Bird's Eye pattern and special burl figures are also available. *Characteristics:* Heavy, hard, strong, and stiff; good shock resistance. *Uses:* Flooring, furniture, boxes and crates, and tool handles. *Finish:* Apply clear finish over bare wood or over light or dark stain.

OAK, American White Oak (*Quercus alba*), Red Oak (*Quercus borealis*). *Source:* Entire eastern United States. *Color and Pattern:* Light grayish brown to reddish brown. Striking grain figure and large, open pores. *Characteristics:* Heavy, strong, and hard; durable under exposure, great wear resistance. *Uses:* Flooring, furniture, watertight cooperage, interior millwork, and boatbuilding. *Finish:* Apply clear finish over bare wood or over light or dark stain.

PECAN (*Carya illinoensis*). *Source:* Southern United States, east of the Mississippi. *Color and Pattern:* Creamy white to reddish brown; occasional dark streaks and large wood pores. *Characteristics:* Very heavy, close grained, hard, and strong. *Uses:* Furniture

and wall paneling. *Finish:* Apply clear finish over bare wood or over light or dark stain.

PINE, White, describes different species from different parts of the country—eastern white pine (punkin pine) for Early American furniture, and western white pine (*pinus monticola*) for most modern pine pieces. They are very similar, although western pine is a little harder. *Color and Pattern:* Cream color to light reddish brown. Visible resin canals and obvious growth rings. *Characteristics:* Moderately light, soft, and stiff; good shock resistance. *Uses:* Construction, boxes and crates, millwork, and furniture (usually reproductions or unfinished). *Finish:* Apply clear finish over bare wood or over light or dark stain. Use sealer before staining. Also consider painting with colored enamel.

POPLAR, Yellow (*Liriodendron tulipifera*), also called Whitewood, Tulipwood. *Source:* New England to Michigan and the Appalachians. *Color and Pattern:* Light yellow to brownish yellow with a greenish tinge. Even texture and straight-grain pattern with barely visible wood pores. *Characteristics:* Medium to light weight; only moderately hard, stiff, and shock resistant. *Uses:* Interior millwork, woodenware, and furniture, where its staining characteristics make it excellent for simulating other woods. *Finish:* Apply clear finish over light or dark stain. Also consider painting with colored enamel.

Wood samples, handy for identifying common furniture woods, can be purchased from mail-order finishing-supply firms

REDWOOD (*Sequoia sempervirens*). *Souce:* California fog belt north of San Francisco to Oregon. *Color and Pattern:* Deep reddish brown with obvious alternating spring and summer growth rings. *Characteristics:* Light, strong, stiff; only moderately hard and marginally shock resistant. Resists decay and termites. *Uses:* Construction, millwork, outdoor furniture. *Finish:* Apply clear finish over bare wood.

ROSEWOOD, Brazilian (*Dalbergia nigra*), other types include East Indian and Honduras Rosewood. *Source:* Brazil, southern India, and Ceylon. *Color and Pattern:* Various shades of dark brown to dark purple; conspicuous black streaks. Large, open wood pores. *Characteristics:* Very heavy, very hard, with an extremely coarse texture. *Uses:* Musical instruments, paneling, furniture, tool handles. *Finish:* Apply clear finish over bare wood.

SYCAMORE, American (*Platanus occidentalis*). *Source:* Maine west to Nebraska and south to eastern Texas and Florida. *Color and Pattern:* Pale reddish brown. Obvious wide growth pattern and small wood pores. *Characteristics:* Moderately heavy and hard; fine textured with good shock resistance. *Uses:* Cooperage, tool handles, hidden parts of furniture. *Finish:* Apply clear finish over bare wood or over stain.

TEAK (*Tectona grandis*). *Source:* Burma, Java, Indo-China, East India. *Color and Pattern:* Tawny yellow to dark brown with frequent lighter and darker streaks. Pattern very similar to that of walnut. *Characteristics:* Heavy, strong, oily, and tough. *Uses:* Paneling, furniture, floors, boatbuilding. *Finish:* Apply clear finish (usually penetrating oil) over bare wood.

WALNUT, American (*Juglans nigra*), also called Black Walnut. *Source:* Vermont to Nebraska and south to Georgia and Texas. *Color and Pattern:* Light gray brown to dark purple brown. Wide variety of plain and highly figured patterns. *Characteristics:* Very strong and stable, only moderately heavy and stiff. Good shock resistance. *Uses:* Furniture, gunstocks, interior trim. *Finish:* Apply clear finish over bare wood. Can be lightly stained.

Chemical removers *are simple to use, safer and more effective than sandpaper for removing old furniture finishes. Do all finish removing in shade, out of direct sun.*

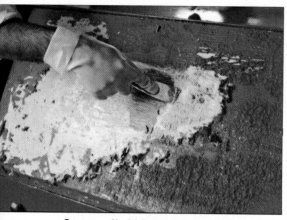

Scrape off old finish *when it loosens and lifts from surface. Flexible putty knife is good for scraping.*

Steel wool *is also useful for finish removal. Wear rubber gloves so steel particles and removing chemicals won't irritate your hands.*

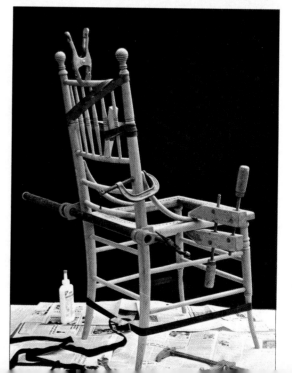

Recycled auto inner tube *strip clamps together glued chair. You can buy or improvise clamps to glue and hold all shaky furniture before further finishing.*

Off with the old finish –on to repair

Tips for stripping & restoring old furniture

Before you apply any new furniture finish, first make sure the wood is ready to receive that finish. The furniture must be structurally solid and ready for many more years of use, and the wood surface must be smooth and clean so the new finish can be applied blemish-free.

The emphasis here, of course, is on quality furniture—furniture that looks its best under a clear final finish. Much of the beauty of older furniture has, over the years, been hidden from view by multiple coats of paint or enamel. Even if you intend to apply more of these opaque finishes to your wood, do yourself a favor and strip off the old finish first—who knows, you may find a genuine antique lurking there.

If your furniture is really old or abused, repairs may be required; even so, always consider removing the old finish so that you can better assess what other work needs to be done.

Removing the old finish

Complete finish removal may not always be necessary—nor is it advisable on very early antiques. Unless the previous finish has been badly damaged or allowed to weather (weathering lessens the ability of the finish to protect the wood), the finish can often be saved with a minimum of restoration (see page 65). On the other hand, if the existing finish is in obviously poor condition, it must first be totally removed.

PICK THE RIGHT WORK AREA

If the weather is agreeable, the natural choice for a place to work might be somewhere outdoors—perhaps by the garage or on the porch or patio. You'll want to put down a lot of newspapers or a large piece of cardboard to keep your work area clean. Don't use plastic painters' tarps for this purpose, for many chemical removers will melt them.

If you think your job might take more than a few days (many refinishing jobs do), choose an indoor work area to protect your furniture from bugs, dust, heat, cold, and rain.

A relatively clean and warm garage or basement would be the logical indoor choice, or you might be able to set aside work space in a family room, laundry, or kitchen.

Whenever you work indoors, be sure you have adequate ventilation; many refinishing chemicals can be hazardous if the vapors are inhaled for long periods of time (see Safety First, page 14).

Chemicals used on furniture are also highly flammable. Do not smoke near finishing products and be careful to properly dispose of all soiled and oily rags.

BEFORE YOU REACH FOR THE SANDPAPER

Sanding may appear to be the quickest and easiest way of removing any old furniture finish. But this is not necessarily so. The trouble with sanding, despite its proven effectiveness, is that you can't remove the old finish without also removing a thin layer of the wood beneath it.

Old wood often acquires a special surface coloration—even under a finish—known as "patina" (see page 6). The impressive beauty of old patina should be saved whenever possible, but if you accidentally remove part of it while sanding, all of it must come off to avoid irregularities in surface color. Loss of patina can detract considerably from the value of a fine old furniture piece.

A sensible alternative is to substitute a good chemical finish remover and steel wool for sandpaper. But before you begin, make sure you know how far you can go without damaging the wood underneath the finish.

If your project is new or unfinished, or if the surface is heavily damaged, do use sandpaper to take off the rough spots and to smooth the wood.

Check for veneers before you begin to strip an old finish. A veneer is a thin piece of fine cabinet wood that is glued over a less distinctive but thicker wood base.

If you look carefully, you will often find telltale signs of veneers along the edges of table tops, cabinet fronts, and drawer sides. If the wood grain is highly figured, always suspect the use of veneers and carefully check the surface for faint lines where the veneers may have been matched together and glued.

Thin veneers can easily be damaged by too much abrasion. Often the striking wood grain is only 1/20 to 1/42 of an inch thick, and you must take great care not to wear the decorative surface right through to the inner-wood core.

Fine wood veneers are used on furniture much more frequently than many people realize. Because high quality hardwoods are scarce, the tendency is to use the wood for veneers to make the most of the short hardwood supply. Since it is often difficult for the home woodworker to be sure whether or not a particular piece has been veneered, always proceed with caution—rely on chemical remover and 1/0 or 2/0 steel wool to remove the old finish.

Remove all hardware before you apply the chemical remover. Knobs, handles, mirrors, and glass and metal ornaments only get in the way while you take the old finish off. Not only might they get potentially damaging chemicals on them but also they are much easier to clean and polish when not attached to the wood.

Dealing with upholstery has its own set of challenges. Removing the old finish around the edges of upholstery is particularly tedious, time-consuming, and—from the point of view of the fabric—risky.

If the upholstery is in good shape and only the wood needs work, play it safe by removing the fabric or having an upholsterer do it for you.

FOR BEST RESULTS — CHEMICAL REMOVERS

Commercial paint removers are the most efficient products for removing all old furniture finishes down to the bare wood.

Paint removers contain a mixture of various chemicals that will soften an old finish and allow its removal by gentle scraping with a putty knife or steel wool. Some removers are designed to be washed away with water, requiring a hard spray from the garden hose to force the old finish from the surface.

Be sure to choose a non-flammable finish remover if you are forced to work anywhere near an open flame, a pilot light, or a motor-driven electric appliance which might cause sparks.

Removing an old finish is always a messy job. If your old furniture finish must be taken off and you would rather not do it yourself, you can probably find professional furniture refinishers who will do the stripping job for you at a reasonable price.

Choosing a chemical remover is largely a matter of weighing cost against convenience. Your choice will depend, too, on what products are locally available to you and on the project you are stripping.

Many experienced refinishers believe that the more costly removers are actually the real bargains because they contain better chemicals and are therefore faster and more efficient.

Safety is a factor, too—inexpensive removers present more of a fire hazard since the chem-

A "safety first" approach

When dealing with potentially harmful wood finishing chemicals and techniques, certain safeguards are in order. Furniture finishing and refinishing is easy, safe, and enjoyable. But before beginning any project, keep in mind these few safety suggestions:

• Be sure to use all chemicals in well-ventilated areas (no closed garages or basements). Avoid breathing any vapors.
• Keep all furniture finishing materials away from children and animals. Many finishing chemicals are caustic; avoid all contact with products on eyes or skin. If an accident occurs, immediately call a physician.
• Paint removers should not be stored for long periods of time. Excessive pressure may build up in unopened cans, causing the fluid to be sprayed on the user when finally opened.
• Never apply finishing chemicals of any kind near an open flame, pilot light, electrical motor, or circuit that may cause open sparks.
• Rags and brushes soaked with furniture finishes are potential fire hazards and should always be cleaned immediately or stored in a safe, well-ventilated place. Do not burn aerosol cans.

icals they contain are usually highly volatile and their flash points are quite low.

Waxes are included in chemical removers to retard evaporation. The cheapest removers contain inexpensive waxes that remain on the wood after the stripping job is done. These waxes must be removed from the surface with lacquer thinner or alcohol; otherwise the new finish won't dry.

A different type of wax—formulated not to stay on the wood—is found in more expensive chemical removers. These removers, which are supposed to leave no residue on the surface, are labeled "no cleanup." You should still use a lacquer thinner or denatured alcohol wash when the remover action is finished to make sure the wood is absolutely bare.

The most expensive paint removers on the market are "water-wash" products. These contain waxes that mix freely with water and rinse away easily. Despite their extra cost, many finishers consider these products a bargain because they are real time-savers. Though these removers are quite easy to use, the water has a potentially damaging effect on any water-soluble glues used in the furniture's construction. Water-wash removers also destroy the colorful surface patina found on valuable antiques.

Chemical removers are available in three consistencies—liquid, semipaste, and paste. If you apply a large quantity of furniture stripper to vertical surfaces, you'll appreciate the thicker consistencies of either semipaste or paste removers. The less a remover drips, the longer it sticks to the surface, the more slowly it evaporates, and the more cutting power it provides in lifting the old finish from the bare wood.

Using a chemical remover correctly requires no extraordinary skill—the most important rule is to use it generously. All removers need to stay on the surface in as thick a layer as possible for a maximum length of time in order to soften the old finish. If insufficient remover is applied, evaporation takes over and all the remover is gone before it has had a chance to work. Pennies saved at this point in scrimping on remover will only cost you dollars of wasted time in the long run.

It's a good idea to wear old clothes and to use quality rubber gloves. Remember to find an out-of-the-way spot (outdoors, preferably, and out of the hot sun) and to put down newspapers to catch the old-finish mess.

It is simple to apply any brand of remover—and produce a good clean job by following these steps:

• *Spread or pour the remover on as thickly as possible,* using a brush with a wooden handle and natural bristles. Many finish-removing chemicals can soften plastic handles and make synthetic bristles useless. Avoid brushing back and forth once the remover is on the surface—such brushing causes faster evaporation and prevents the chemicals from doing their job.

• *If the surface seems too dull* or if there isn't enough remover in certain spots, only then should you brush on more. Begin by keeping the whole surface wet and letting the remover do all the work for you.

• *Before a half-hour has passed,* check to see that the thick coating you've applied has done its work—the chemical action is completed when the old finish appears wrinkled and "lifted" and is softened all the way through to the wood. Then take a pad of coarse steel wool and a flexible putty knife (be careful not

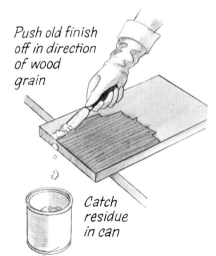

Push old finish off in direction of wood grain

Catch residue in can

to gouge the wood) and gently slide the old finish off the surface in the direction of the grain.

If you're using a water-wash remover and you're sure the piece has no delicate veneers with old

glues that will loosen in water, you can rinse your project off with the garden hose as an alternative to the preceding step. The water, however, will take away any patina that the wood might have, and it will raise the grain.

Cleaning up the newly stripped wood will probably convince you that even the most careful application of a chemical remover will leave some remnants of the old finish on the surface or in the grain. If you've used an inexpensive remover, you might even find a film of wax coating the wood. These residual effects must be removed or they will interfere with later staining and final finishing.

Wait for the stripped project to dry slightly before inspecting for any residue. For large areas, 2/0 steel wool and lacquer thinner or denatured alcohol (shellac-thinner grade) will do an excellent cleanup job. For small areas around carvings, moldings, corners, or detail of any kind, try using cotton swabs, old dental tools, an ice pick, or an old toothbrush with the same solvent. These tools are indispensable for getting into hard-to-reach places.

To remove loosened finish from small areas such as carvings or moldings, use toothpicks or moist cotton swabs

If there is much old-finish residue on your piece, either apply more chemical remover or sand lightly with 180-grit or finer sandpaper. The removal of every kind of finish is subject to different procedures, depending on the number of coats, the wood underneath, and the type of remover used. Be prepared to adjust your techniques to the demands of the specific task.

New life for damaged wood

As soon as the old finish has been totally removed, analyze the wood surface to make sure that it's ready for smoothing. Often you'll find repairs are needed, especially on older pieces of furniture. Begin by looking for the most common signs of disrepair—loose drawers, broken or missing chair pieces, cracked table tops, and fractured legs. Look also for deep gouges, dents, or blemishes on the surface where they will detract from the final refinished effect.

The majority of furniture repairs are not difficult to make if you have the patience and a few of the proper tools. Clamps, files, sandpaper, and glue are all fairly common household items—or should be for any householder who likes to work with wood. A rubber mallet and an electric drill might also be wise investments.

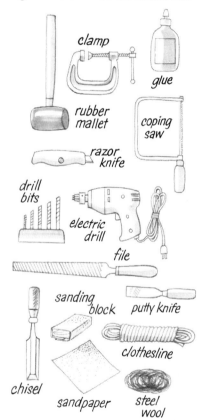

clamp
glue
rubber mallet
coping saw
razor knife
drill bits
electric drill
file
sanding block
putty knife
clothesline
chisel
sandpaper
steel wool

Because many of the repairs require sanding and further smoothing after completion, making all your repairs before you begin sanding will mean that you'll have to do the job only once.

All furniture repair must begin with a determination of exactly what work needs to be done. Any structural damage that is not fixed before refinishing will only shorten the life of the newly refinished furniture once it's put into use. Surface blemishes that may seem to be hardly worth repairing will be emphasized and intensified when you apply a stain and a final clear finish to the wood. For this reason, you should be sure to correct minor as well as major damages.

To simplify furniture repairs, divide whatever work needs to be done into three classifications: regluing, replacing parts, and repairing the surface.

• *Disassemble and reglue* all joints, drawers, spindles, backs, arms, and legs that have loosened. Glue and clamp all cracks in the wood.

• Replace any missing wooden parts—shattered table tops, unrepairable chair legs and arms, decorative moldings, leg supports, feet, or wooden knobs. Make sure all wooden repairs are in place before the final wood smoothing.

• *Repair gouges, dents, surface blemishes,* and all minor imperfections. In many cases, some of these small repairs will have to be made after the first coat of stain is applied to ensure that the color of the repair matches the color of the stained wood.

HOW TO REPAIR LOOSE JOINTS AND CRACKED WOOD

Loose joints and cracks should be the first things you fix. When a joint is loose or wood is cracked, movement is caused in other furniture parts, resulting in still more loose joints. If not corrected, one loose joint could eventually cause your entire piece of furniture to fall apart.

Choose the right glue from among the many modern adhesives on the market today. If your gluing needs are simple, like a loose chair spindle or leg, use a common white glue that needs no mixing and is easy to apply. Or you may prefer a "yellow" glue (aliphatic resin glue), which is

similar to white glue but offers a slightly quicker drying time and a slightly stronger hold.

These modern glues are far more useful than many of the old animal and fish-derived glues that hold most old furniture pieces together. As many modern glues dry, chemical changes make them impervious to water and even to moisture in the air.

When gluing problems are greater—such as a cracked chair leg that will undergo much stress—stronger glues are called for.

Plastic resin, resorcinol resin, and epoxy glues all require mixing but guarantee a final glued joint that is often stronger than the wood itself. Because they are inconvenient to prepare and the resulting bond is permanent, you'll want to use them only when their great strength is needed. When using these stronger glues, follow manufacturer's instructions for mixing, application, and drying time to ensure adequate strength.

Disassemble your furniture whenever possible before making repairs. Carefully remove all screws (watch for concealed fastenings) and knock glued sections apart with a rubber or rawhide-faced hammer. Lightly clean away all old glue from the individual pieces—use sandpaper, a coarse file, a knife, or hot water. Any old glue that remains will inhibit the bonding of the new glue.

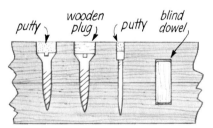

putty — wooden plug — putty — blind dowel

Types of concealed fastenings

To disassemble loose joints, use a soft-faced mallet

If an old joint is loose but you can't get it completely apart without damage to the surrounding wood, use a hypodermiclike glue injector (available at hardware and craft stores) to squirt a little thin glue behind the joint where it will do the most good.

Various products are also available that swell the wood fibers. If successful, the swelling technique of fixing a loose joint makes both gluing and disassembly of the furniture piece unnecessary. These wood-swelling products can be useful, provided the joints are not so loose that the wood can't swell enough. Because there is a limit to just how much wood fibers can swell, wood-swelling techniques are useful only when the void in the socket is fairly small.

Be careful to wash away any wood-swelling chemicals that may get on the surface for they are likely to react unfavorably when mixed with other finishing chemicals at some later stage in the refinishing process.

When a socket becomes unusually large for its spindle (because of continual movement and wear), no amount of glue will fill the void and lock the joint together. All oversize sockets must

be plugged and then rebored to fit the smaller original spindle. To do this, obtain a hardwood dowel of the same diameter as the socket, glue it carefully in place, and then bore another hole, using a drill bit of the same diameter as the spindle for a perfectly tight fit.

Repair cracks in table tops, drawers, and chair seats before they crack any further. If the two sections on either side of the crack have not totally separated, it may be possible to work glue down into the opening by rocking the two sections back and forth with your hands; a glue injector is another possibility.

Once the glue has been applied, gently open and close the crack to force the glue into voids where it's needed most. Then apply a clamp across the width of the wood to keep the crack closed while the glue has a chance to dry. Wash or wipe off all excess glue.

If the crack in a table or chair leg is very bad, a new piece may have to be made. However, many broken furniture legs can be quite satisfactorily repaired, even if they must be strong enough to support considerable weight. But these furniture parts that receive much stress must be thoroughly repaired if they are not to break again.

When cracks are simple with-the-grain fractures, the pieces will usually fit back together quite well, and simple gluing and clamping may be all that is needed. If you feel that gluing alone can't support the weight of a particular furniture piece, insert a dowel into both sides of the cracked area for additional stability and strength.

Sometimes cracks will occur across the wood grain, and wood fibers will become so completely torn that the two pieces will not easily fit together again. In this case, you may have no choice but to replace the broken part entirely. Or you might try gluing the pieces together as best you can and then placing an additional supporting splint across the crack in some location where it won't be noticed.

You also might try to fix severe breaks, by cutting the cracked portion entirely away, fitting a new insert in its place with dowels on both sides, and gluing. When

Three ways to repair a broken leg so it will support weight

1. Bore holes on either side of break, insert dowel, and glue

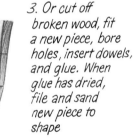

2. Or cut out a recess where it won't show, make a matching splint, glue splint and break together, and sand to shape

3. Or cut off broken wood, fit a new piece, bore holes, insert dowels, and glue. When glue has dried, file and sand new piece to shape

your newly repaired section is dry, camouflage it to match any existing decorative details.

Never glue without clamping, since all newly glued joints require some form of pressure while they are drying if the best possible bond is to be achieved. Hardware stores carry many varieties of woodworking clamps that are handy to use. These clamps are usually quite expensive, though, and the creative home refinisher will find that many common household objects will work just as well.

Sometimes you can get all the pressure you need from a stack of heavy books (use a sheet of wax paper to protect the books from excess glue). Or you might try a few loops of clothesline or cut-up

To correct an oversize socket...

1. Check to see how much larger hole is than spindle size

2. Glue and insert solid wood plug into hole

3. Bore new plug to spindle size

inner tubes, wrapped around the furniture and twisted tight with a stick. With a little imagination, any number of pressure-producing devices are possible, depending on the particular clamping problem at hand.

WHEN TO REPLACE MISSING WOOD

If a piece of wood is too badly broken to be repaired—or if a piece is missing entirely—replacement is the only solution. First decide whether your furniture piece is really worth all the time you will spend restoring it to its original condition. If only one or two minor pieces of wood are missing and the style of the piece particularly appeals to you, then go ahead and try your hand at furniture reconstruction. Major projects, though, are often best left to the experts.

Retain all decorative detail if you attempt to do the repair job yourself. A restored piece of furniture should look much as it did originally. Because antique moldings and period designs contribute greatly to old furniture's authenticity, you'll want to work carefully and take all the time you need to do a good job.

Begin by finding the right kind of wood to match your particular furniture. Many types of wood are quite difficult to locate today, and it's often hard—even when you do find the specific type you require—to match up a newly sawn piece with an older piece of the same species (see wood characteristics, pages 8-9).

Many standard cabinet woods are available newly sawn in good lumberyards, or you can order them from large mail-order supply firms that cater to craftsmen. Whenever possible, try to save odds and ends of uncommon woods. Hardwoods are probably the most valuable, but softwoods—particularly old, wide pine boards with a beautiful patina—are often worth their weight in gold.

With luck, you could find wood for your repair needs right around your home. A leftover leaf from an old oak, walnut, or mahogany dining table that you may have sold years ago can be just right for nearly any major or minor repair. If you need hickory for a chair spindle, look around for an old ax

or sledge-hammer handle. Ash can often be found in old rake handles, and birch is used in most broom handles.

Fitting a new piece into existing furniture often takes ingenuity. For instance, how do you replace a spindle that fits into a socket at both ends, unless you completely disassemble the furniture? Solve this particular problem by making the new part in two pieces with a tapered splice across the center. After fitting a part into the socket at each end, simply glue and clamp the splice together.

To repair a broken spindle without disassembling chair...

1. Make a new spindle slightly longer than original one and cut it diagonally in center

2. Remove broken pieces, insert new spindle in each hole, glue joint, wrap with clothesline, and clamp until dry

Coping with warped boards doesn't necessarily involve replacing them. Warping problems are frequently not permanent; often repair rather than replacement is the solution. All warps result when wood fibers on one side of a board contain more moisture than those on the other side.

Before replacing warped wood, always try to repair it by drying out the convex side or by adding more moisture to the concave side. You can do this easily by placing the wood, concave side down, on wet grass under the hot sun for a few days. Even the most curved boards may straighten out again.

Replacing missing veneer is a job for the experts—it often is more difficult than reveneering the entire piece of furniture from scratch. The main difficulty is to find new veneer that matches the wood species and grain of the original veneer.

Instead of searching for a new piece, use a little glue on the end of a toothpick and try to repair the loose, lifting, or blistered veneer that is still fairly intact. Weight the veneer down with books (use wax paper to protect them from glue), and stain and finish the repaired area if necessary.

HOW TO PATCH DENTS AND DEFECTS

Much old furniture is structurally sound with only a few scrapes, scratches, or nicks to reveal the amount of use it has received. Even a new piece of unfinished furniture may have marks to show for the time it spent on a furniture dealer's display floor. A certain "distressed" look (see Distressing, page 52) is evident on all pieces of wood, regardless of origin or age—it's something that can't be helped. Indeed, the value of many antiques is enhanced by the "wear" marks that prove authenticity.

Some high-use areas of a piece of furniture are more subtly distressed than others—for example, it won't require too practiced an eye to observe that separate places on a dining table have been worn away by countless elbows or that table legs have been made smooth and shiny from the abrasion of numerous feet. Very little can or should be done to cover up such signs of actual wear, but scratches, nicked corners, and surface dents are best repaired before a new furniture finish is applied.

Dents are found on nearly every piece of well-used furniture. If the bruise is shallow, you may be able to return the compressed wood fibers to their original condition by wetting them with water to make them swell. For proper moisture penetration, of course, be sure that all wood finish is removed from around the surface of the dent.

When water alone won't raise a dent, place a damp cloth and the tip of a heated clothing iron over the dent for a few seconds and again watch for the wood fibers to swell. You may have to do this several times, a few seconds at a time. When the grain in the dent has risen to the level of the surrounding surface, remove the iron and cloth and prepare the rest of the surface for sanding.

Scars and nicks always result in the loss of some wood. These blemishes can be filled with one of the three standbys of the home wood finisher—wood dough, wood putty, or plastic wood. These three products are easy to work with when you plan to use an enamel finish, but they are often difficult to use under a clear finish.

Problems arise when you begin to stain the newly repaired wood. Because all patching materials have a different rate of absorption from that of the surrounding wood pores, the patching materials often end up darker or lighter than you intended. To avoid this discrepancy, try to select wood-patching materials that most closely resemble the color of your final finish. A little experimentation will save you much time and effort. One way to experiment would be to apply a few patching products of different colors to an out-of-the-way spot on your furniture piece. By applying a stain—and possibly a final finish—to this sample area, you can get an idea how the repair will blend in with the surrounding wood.

Listed by decreasing degree of absorption, these are the most popular patching materials:

• *Wood dough* is a fairly absorbent patching material, easy to apply and usually able to absorb quite a bit of oil stain after it dries. It comes in a number of popular wood-tone colors. Yet, making these original colors, once they have been covered with stain, match the color of your wood surface is something you will have to experiment with. Always choose the color closest to your final finish.

• *Wood putty* comes in two varieties—a premixed form in a can and a powdered form that you mix with water. Premixed is excellent for small imperfections (nail holes and molding joints); the water-mix variety is good for larger voids.

Both putties are available primarily in a creamy white color, and both take oil and water stains reasonably well. For the best color match, most finishers who use the water-mix putty extensively color it with wood-tone dyes and pigments as they mix it. As with other products, you should be sure to read the manufacturer's label for mixing instructions.

• *Plastic wood* is hard and nonabsorbent—very little stain will penetrate it. It is available in numerous colors. Again, it's worthwhile to experiment in order to pick a color that most closely resembles your final wood finish.

With a putty knife, apply the patching material to all the scarred and nicked areas. Be sure to compress it firmly into the voids to guarantee good adhesion. Patching materials will often look darker than the surrounding wood while you are applying them. When dry and sanded, though, patching materials will tend to appear lighter than the wood, only to turn dark again under a final finishing coat.

To repair a scar on the wood surface...

1. Apply wood patch of your choice with a flexible putty knife

2. Sand surface smooth when patch is dry; if necessary, spot-stain the repair to match surrounding wood

Though many patching materials are labeled "nonshrinking," you'll achieve best results on very large voids if you use more than one application. Be sure to let each layer dry thoroughly before you apply the next. Also, leave each layer a little higher than the

surrounding surface. When the patch hardens, if it hasn't shrunk to size you can always sand to blend it in with the surrounding wood.

Gouges often go considerably deeper than simple scars and nicks. In many cases you will have to use small pieces of wood to replace areas that are too large to be corrected by any other method.

When repairing the damaged corner of a table, cut out both the defect and the new piece of scrap wood at the same angle and glue in place. When the new piece has dried, the repair should be shaped to match the surrounding wood.

To repair a nicked corner...

1. First cut corner off diagonally and glue a new piece of matching wood in its place

2. Clamp the piece securely by any convenient method and, when glue is dry, shape new corner so it matches surrounding wood

To repair smaller gashes, such as those found on the edges of table legs, glue a new piece of wood into the indentation. Let the repair dry thoroughly; then file or plane away any excess wood.

Regardless of how badly damaged a wood surface appears, nearly all furniture can be restored to refinishable shape with only a little practice, some careful thought, and a few woodworking tools.

How to prepare the wood surface

A guide to sanding, sealing, & bleaching

Proper surface preparation is the key to any successful final wood finish. Whether your specific piece of furniture needs finishing or refinishing, once you've properly prepared the wood surface, the remaining steps are really very much alike.

If your furniture already has a finish that's old or damaged and can't be easily repaired (see page 65), remove it according to the steps outlined on page 13. Once you have removed the old finish down to the bare wood, simply smooth away any residual trace of the old finish and prepare the surface as if the wood were new.

If the wood *is* new, though, and has no finish on it, follow the specific instructions for bare wood surfaces outlined in this chapter. Look for special hints for finishing unfinished furniture on pages 24-25.

Final furniture finishes are only as beautiful as the wood over which they are applied. Take a tip from the pros: spend that extra effort on your bare wood surface—smoothing, bleaching, and sealing; you'll be glad you did.

Smoothing the wood

Smoothing—with sandpaper or steel wool—is the most important operation in preparing a wood surface for a finish.

You might spend many hours staining, finishing, and polishing, but if the beginning surface has any trace of roughness, the final reflective finish will only emphasize all the bad points. By taking time to do a good job of sanding, you can make unwanted tool marks, water marks, blemishes, traces of the old finish, and other surface irregularities disappear, giving the surface a finish of professional quality and appearance.

SANDPAPER OR STEEL WOOL?

Long a blessing to the home woodworker, sandpaper seems to inspire overuse. Knowing when not to use sandpaper—with its highly abrasive qualities—is just as important as knowing when to use it. In seconds, the heavy hand of a careless refinisher using sandpaper can destroy the distinctive tool marks and beautiful patina of an early American dresser. For those situations where too much sanding could be harmful (with classic antiques and veneers, for example), steel wool is the answer. Some professional refinishers use nothing else.

Sandpaper acquired its name many years ago when heavy paper was actually coated with abrasive particles of sand. Today, types of sandpaper for use on furniture can be classified by the four different minerals that make them up. Two of the minerals are natural, coming from mines or quarries, and two are artificially produced in electric furnaces.

The numbers printed on the back of sandpaper indicate the coarseness or fineness of the abrasive —the higher the number, the finer the abrasive particles (see Which Abrasive to Use?, page 23). At almost any paint or hardware store, you should be

Sand or steel wool *wood thoroughly to remove all traces of old finish. Adequate sanding eliminates wood irregularities, provides even surface and open wood pores for staining, filling, and other finishing steps.*

Bleaching *can remove discoloration from open wood pores and grain. Oxalic acid is useful here for removing weathered dark spots from this old oak chair.*

Strip-sand spindles *and other turned objects with long strip of sandpaper. Choose fine abrasive grit to leave few sanding marks. Push and pull with "shoeshine" movement of your wrists.*

able to find flint, garnet, aluminum oxide, or silicon carbide sandpaper:

• *Flint quartz* (generally called "flint") sandpaper is usually off-white. Commonly found in hardware stores, this paper is dull, cuts the wood slowly, clogs easily, and quickly loses its grit. Though initially inexpensive to buy, it will end up costing you more than any of the other papers in terms of your time and temper, as well as of final surface quality.

• *Garnet* is reddish and is the most popular abrasive for both amateur and professional wood finishing. This excellent paper has two major things going for it—it is hard and sharp enough to cut well when new, and the particles of grit can fracture enough through use to offer new, unused cutting edges to the surface you are sanding.

• *Aluminum oxide,* reddish brown to gray black, is made in electric furnaces where very high temperatures fuse the mineral bauxite into a uniform abrasive. Stocked by better paint, hardware, and craft stores, this paper has toughness and enduring sharpness that make it one of the most versatile for the wood finisher. Whenever possible, try to purchase "open coat" aluminum oxide paper—it is less densely coated with grit, which means less clogging and extended paper life.

• *Silicon carbide* is a black, hard, and sharp abrasive produced by high-temperature fusing of silica sand and coke—much like the way nature makes a diamond. Its superior cutting ability is useful for the final sanding of lacquers, plastics, composition materials, and metals.

Steel wool is most popular for smoothing off newly stripped wood surfaces and for light buffing between finish coats. Purchased in the form of pads and available in many grades, steel wool is especially attractive to the woodworker for its versatility.

Grade 1/0, the most common of all, is used chiefly for general cleaning and smoothing—particularly after finish removers have done their job. Grades 2/0 and 3/0 are finely textured and are often used for final surface smoothing before finish application. Grade 4/0 has a very fine texture and is perfect for smoothing between final finishing coats.

MECHANICAL OR HAND SANDING?

All sanding can be done by hand or by machine. A power sander undoubtedly provides the fastest sanding, but you should practice handling one before using it for fine furniture work. Sanding by hand is slower but safer, allowing more sensitivity to the wood's surface irregularities. Hand sanding with a sanding block often results in a much smoother final product.

Types of power sanders

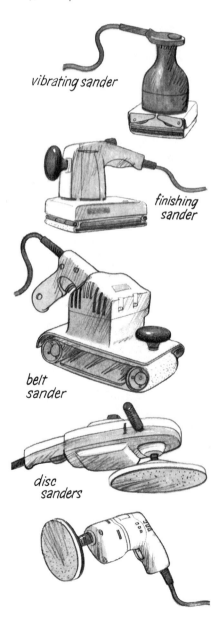

vibrating sander

finishing sander

belt sander

disc sanders

Power sanders include four main types—vibrating sanders, finishing sanders, belt sanders, and disc sanders.

• *Vibrating sanders* give very short, fast, orbital or in-line strokes that result in beautifully smoothed surfaces. Though excellent for final sanding, they are extremely slow for heavier work where leveling is required.

• *Finishing sanders* are the best for all-around use. They operate in one of three ways: straight-line, orbital, or dual action.

With straight-line action, the abrasive paper moves back and forth in the direction the sander is moved. Primarily used for sanding with the grain, this sander doesn't remove much material, but the end result is smooth and pleasing.

With the orbital-action sander, the abrasive moves in a flat, small oval rather than straight back and forth. Because movement is across the grain, more material is removed from the wood surface, but swirl marks made by the sandpaper grit leave their imprint. In order to complete the job, you must sand away these swirls.

Dual-action finishing sanders combine both straight-line and orbital actions in the same machine. You can begin sanding with the orbital action for maximum wood removal if you need it, and then turn a key for straight-line sanding and a perfect final finish.

• *Belt sanders* are the fastest straight-line sanders around—the abrasive constantly moves against the wood on a continuously revolving belt. Though more difficult to use than a finishing sander, a belt sander can be an extremely useful tool; you'll master its use with a little practice. It can rough-sand large quantities of flat material or even strip off old finishes from table tops without the application of chemical remover.

• *Disc sanders* are not recommended for delicate sanding of furniture. Both the large commercial kind and the small ones that can be attached to a power drill are hard to handle, and they remove too much material too quickly. In addition, disc sanders leave large, cross-grain sanding marks that are difficult to remove. Fitted with a buffing pad, though, these sanders are excellent for buffing the high gloss on wax.

Hand sanding is still the traditionally preferred method for smoothing wood surfaces. Even though rapid power sanding does a good job in most cases, many wood finishing experts recommend that the very last sanding be done by hand. For successful hand sanding, provide some form of backing support other than the fingers or hand. One way to get this extra support is to use a sanding block, available at paint and hardware stores in various sizes and styles—or you can make your own.

Commercial blocks range from simple, flat blocks of wood, metal, plastic, or rubber to automatic, self-feeding sanding tools that contain rolls of sandpaper in the handles.

Sanding blocks are easy to make at home—just wrap the abrasive around a wood block faced with a 1/2-inch-thick sheet of sponge rubber or felt. Don't attempt to use unpadded blocks for finish sanding—if a piece of grit or dust gets between the block and the paper, it can produce a high spot that heats up, clogs, and causes scratches across the surface you are trying to smooth.

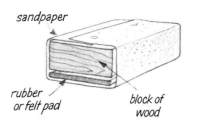

Make your own sanding block...

sandpaper

rubber or felt pad

block of wood

SURFACE SANDING TECHNIQUES

Begin by examining the piece to be smoothed in a good light to locate all major defects that appear on the surface.

If the previous finish of your furniture has just been removed or if the wood surface is otherwise in bad shape, choose a fairly coarse abrasive (100 to 150 grit) and sand the surface cautiously at a slight angle to the wood's grain. This will level the ridges and remove any chemical residue, glue stains, or other discolorations, but it will also leave small scratches over the entire surface of your project.

Follow this initial sanding with a medium-grit abrasive (180 to 220 grit), this time sanding with the

grain. Take your time and work carefully; any major across-the-grain scratches made at this point may be magnified later by a final clear finish. Continue this second step until all the small scratches produced by the first sanding have been removed.

Between sandings, remember to wipe the project off thoroughly with a rag slightly moistened with paint thinner—a few stray, coarse grits can ruin the finely sanded surface you're trying to achieve.

Finally, change to a fine grade of abrasive paper (240 to 320 grit) and again sand directly with the grain. Use long, even strokes with your hand firmly grasping the sanding block. By this time the surface should be approaching a high degree of smoothness. To check for smoothness, place a light behind the surface and bend down to observe the light's reflection. Go over any high spots or other irregularities you might find, and then check the surface at least once more.

Before the final sanding with very fine finishing paper, some professional finishers like to apply a very thin "wash" coat of shellac (see Sealers, page 27) or any

(Continued on page 26)

Which abrasive to use?

Listed in the chart at right are the most popular abrasive paper grit sizes and their uses. All papers are graded by the size of their cutting grits. Higher grit numbers mean smaller grit sizes, resulting in the removal of less wood surface with each motion of the cutting teeth. On some brands of abrasive paper, grit numbers range from 12 to 600 (600 being the finest). Other abrasives are labeled by "0" numbers (0, 2/0, 3/0, etc.) or grit descriptions (fine, medium, etc.).

For professional results, you should sand hardwoods *in sequence* with each listed abrasive grade, but you need only to sand softwoods with one representative paper grade from each category. If you skip more than a few grit sizes on the way to a finished hardwood product, using an abrasive too fine to do the job may take you more sanding time in the long run.

Sanding blocks are useful whenever sanding flat surfaces. When abrasive paper is held in the hand, undue sanding pressure is applied to the surface by the finger tips and the hand's palm. A padded sanding block equalizes the

hand's pressure on the abrasive and ensures a smooth, flat, even surface.

	Grit Size	Symbol
Coarse Sandpaper		
Initial smoothing	40	1-1/2
and shaping of	50	1
unfinished wood	60	1/2
	80	0
Medium Sandpaper	100	2/0
Intermediate smoothing	120	3/0
on all fine furniture	150	4/0
surfaces		
Fine Sandpaper	180	5/0
Final smoothing on all	220	6/0
hard and soft bare	240	7/0
wood surfaces	280	8/0
Very Fine Sandpaper	320	9/0
Wet-sanding and	360	—
between-coat sanding	400	10/0
of final finishes	500	—
	600	—

Unfinished furniture

Purchasing unfinished furniture can often be an inexpensive alternative to the high cost of furnishing your home. Unfinished furniture is available in a wide variety of styles, qualities, and prices. But you should always check carefully to make sure you are getting the top species of wood and the sound construction you're supposedly paying for (see Know Your Wood, pages 8-9).

Pine is probably the single most widely used wood for unfinished furniture, although many other woods are also available. As with many fast-growing conifers, pine has a wild and irregular grain. Because of these irregularities, it may be wise first to use a sealer of cut shellac (see Sealers, page 27) before staining. Always experiment first on a hidden surface to obtain the effect that you want. Hardwoods, of course, will usually need no sealer, and you are assured of an excellent finish with nearly any of the available modern wood finishing products.

Choosing unfinished furniture *can be fun for entire family. More stores are now selling furniture of this type—look for their addresses in Yellow Pages under "Furniture—Unfinished."*

1. Carefully sand *any piece of furniture before finishing it. Start with 180-grit or finer abrasive. Pieces of nude furniture are often not sanded nearly as well as they need to be when you buy them.*

2. Seal furniture *if necessary. Soft woods and plywoods will benefit from light wood sealer applied before staining. On harder woods, a sealer often seals too well, preventing stain from penetrating.*

3. Strip-sand *to avoid flat spots on spindles when you sand again after sealing. Be sure to go over all parts of wood thoroughly—final finish can only be as good as the surface to which it's applied.*

4. Stain your furniture *with rag or brush—brush will insure even stain penetration into various crevices and details. Then wipe excess off with clean rag. Let surface dry before further finishing.*

5. Pour on penetrating resin—*or you may need added protection of thick polyurethane varnish. If you pour out a generous amount to begin with, you won't have to reach for the can every time your rag or brush runs dry.*

6. Wipe penetrating resin *evenly over your project's surface. Again, you may need to use brush to ensure adequate coverage. When finish dries, rub it gently with fine steel wool and wax for even greater protection.*

...Continued from page 23

commercial sanding sealer applied as directed by the manufacturer.

As a substitute method, dampen the wood slightly with a water-moistened sponge, causing the grain to raise and the wood fibers to stand up. After the wood dries, sand the raised grain smooth, and the surface will be ready for further finishing. Both "wash" methods stiffen and eliminate tiny wood fibers and give a smoother surface look.

For smoothing between coats of a final finish such as varnish, shellac, lacquer, or enamel, try wet sanding. It will generally give the best results. Be sure to use extremely fine waterproof abrasive paper (either aluminum oxide or silicon carbide) and wet the paper frequently to lubricate the abrasive action and to help prevent clogging of the grit. Best wetting agents are water (but not on shellac, which is discolored by water), mineral spirits, kerosene, and rubbing oil. Use the same waterproof paper for the final rubbing of your complete finish.

STEEL WOOL—A SAFE CHOICE

Steel wool is probably most useful when the furniture you are working on has a beautiful old patina or has been veneered. Veneers require careful smoothing to avoid cutting through to the core stock. Since on veneers it is often impossible to follow the grain of the wood, steel wool, with its low cutting capacity, is usually the only choice.

Use the finer grades of steel wool, such as 2/0 and 3/0, and avoid too much rubbing in any one spot. Apply only light pressure to the surface and clean off all small particles of steel with a cloth dampened with paint thinner—not too wet or you may loosen the glues holding the delicate veneers in place.

Steel wool is also perfect for general smoothing on irregular surfaces, such as those found on carvings and turnings (table or chair legs, for example). It is easy to use (wear rubber gloves to keep your fingers safe from bits of steel), and it won't disturb the patina or tooling marks left by old-world craftsmen—the very characteristics that make some antiques so valuable.

Color control by bleaching

Bleaching is the process of lightening the color of a wood by the use of chemicals. Useful in furniture finishing for removing or lightening color in specific areas (or entire surfaces) before a new color is applied, bleaching allows dark wood to be finished lighter or removes dark stain that has not been completely stripped from previously finished furniture.

THE THREE TYPES OF BLEACH

For furniture use there are basically three types of bleach. They are (from weakest to strongest) chlorinated laundry bleach; oxalic acid; and commercial, two-solution wood bleach.

Chlorinated liquid laundry bleach is comparatively weak and is good for slight to moderate lightening. Repeated applications remove similar amounts of color, giving you some degree of control in bleaching mottled or stained areas of wood. When used full strength, laundry bleach is excellent for removing chemical, dye, ink, and water stains from wood surface.

Oxalic acid is the best bleach to use not only on many natural wood colors but also on many water and chemical stains. It is a mild bleach when used alone; if you need something more effective, follow it with a solution of sodium hyposulfite (photographer's type).

To prepare a standard oxalic acid solution, dissolve 3 ounces of oxalic acid crystals in 1 quart of hot water. For milder bleaching, oxalic acid may be used in a weaker solution if necessary.

If you need the extra bleaching strength of a second solution, mix 3 ounces of hyposulfite in 1 quart of water and apply to the still-wet surface.

Two-solution bleaches are fairly expensive and extremely strong. Because of their strength, they can bring out really light tones on dark woods, something no other type of bleach can do.

Follow instructions closely and don't take short cuts—potentially dangerous chemicals are involved. Since ingredients and instructions vary from product to product, keep a close watch on the bleaching process and carefully follow manufacturer's directions. In a two-solution bleach, the first liquid is often a caustic alkali; the second, usually an extremely strong hydrogen peroxide.

HOW TO APPLY BLEACH

When applying bleaches remember they are all concentrated chemical solutions that can burn any flesh or clothing with which they come in contact. Rubber gloves and old clothes are always a good precaution. Under all circumstances keep these liquids away from the mouth and eyes. If any bleach should accidentally get on the skin, wash it off at once with large quantities of water.

Begin by making sure that the surface to be bleached is smooth and free of all grease, old finish, and wax. Since best bleaching results are obtained by uniform bleach penetration, it is always a good idea to go over the surface with fine sandpaper to open the wood pores before you begin. And since all bleach contains water and will raise the wood grain slightly, you should be prepared to do more light sanding when the bleaching job is completed (see Safety, page 14).

To apply bleach, use only a *synthetic nylon* brush; you'll find that natural bristles are not compatible with the various chemical ingredients. Brush on all forms of bleach in the direction of the wood grain to prevent unequal absorption and irregular lightening. Apply all materials evenly; don't try to saturate or flood the surface to speed the process along.

All chemicals leave some residue on the wood surface. When bleaching is completed, this residue should be neutralized with a borax and water wash.

Mix up your borax wash (1 cup borax per quart of hot water) and apply the rapidly cooling solution to the wood's surface. Then rinse the wood with clear water, wipe, and allow the wood to dry thoroughly—about 24 hours if it's in a warm room—before attempting further finishing.

If you try to sand before thoroughly neutralizing the residue, invest in a lightweight painter's mask to protect yourself from any airborne pollutants.

For bleaching with oxalic acid...

1. Mix oxalic crystals with warm water

2. Apply bleach in direction of wood grain

3. Neutralize wood surface with borax and water before sanding

Sealing the surface

"Sealer" is an ambiguous wood finishing term that refers to any product capable of sealing (or partially sealing) the wood's pores. Whether or not you use a sealer is largely a matter of personal preference, but if your furniture has been carefully sanded and prepared, the proper use of a good wood sealer will almost guarantee professional results.

WHEN TO SEAL A SURFACE

Generally, it's a good idea to seal both the stain coat and wood filler (see Filling, page 32) on first-class work. Sealer coats, however, should never be applied so heavily as to leave no room in the pores for further finishing. Properly applied, a "wash" coat of sealer over a stain is invisible. Here are points that will help you to understand sealer's versatility:

• Sealers are to clear finishes what undercoats are to paint. They provide an excellent surface for the final finish to adhere to.

• Sealers can harden soft areas of wood surfaces and allow a more accurate and thorough final sanding.

• Sealers can tame the wild grains of softwoods—especially plywood—because they allow a much more uniform stain penetration. Test the entire procedure on a hidden part of the furniture or on a

scrap of the same type of wood. Don't use synthetic sealers—they are impervious to stain.

Shellac is the easiest sealer to use. Mix equal parts of 4-pound cut shellac and denatured alcohol; then apply. After it dries, sand lightly with fine sandpaper and then apply an oil or pigmented stain. Try both types of stain with different ratios of shellac and alcohol to get the appearance that you want.

• Sealers prevent stains and fillers from bleeding through into the final finishing coats.

WHICH SEALER IS WHICH?

Wood finishers have never completely agreed on the best type of sealer to use under successive finishing coats. Today it is generally believed that the sealer should be a greatly thinned-down version of whatever product is used for the final finish.

Shellac has been recognized for many years as the standard undercoater for use under varnish, shellac, lacquer, or paint. White shellac is used for light finishes and orange shellac for browns and mahoganies. Mix 1 part of pure shellac (4-pound cut) with 8 parts of denatured alcohol for a stain sealer. Or mix 1 part of shellac to 4 parts of alcohol for use over a filler. (See page 38 for details on how to cut shellac.)

If your final finish is a natural-oil varnish and you have no shellac on hand, you can still make an excellent sealer—mix 1 part of varnish with 1 part of pure turpentine. This procedure, though, will not work with the special synthetic varnishes (if the label indicates that your varnish can be thinned with turpentine, you can be sure it is not synthetic). Synthetic varnishes and penetrating resins need no sealer.

Another popular sealer for lacquer and varnish is a special product sold in paint stores and known as "sanding sealer." As the name implies, it is effective for final sanding and has a petroleum/chemical base that dries ready-to-sand in about an hour. It brushes easily, dries with an exceptionally hard surface, and contains a sanding agent that makes the wood fibers stand up, permitting clean, powdery sanding without gumming the paper.

APPLYING SEALER

For best results, sealer coats should be as thin as possible. Brush on only one coat at a time; sealer should flow onto the wood easily and dry quickly. Be sure to read the manufacturer's instructions on the label—application methods may differ with different brands. Sand carefully when dry.

Oak furniture has character all its own. Leave it natural or stain it any color from golden oak through dark oak to walnut or red mahogany.

1. Staining *a piece of furniture is simple. Wipe or brush on your chosen stain.*

2. Rubbing the stain *around the surface in a circular motion insures even overall penetration.*

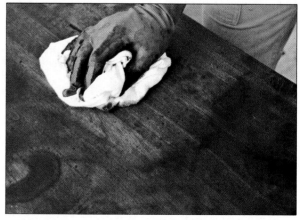

3. Wiping it off *with a clean rag in the direction of the grain completes the job. Wear protective gloves.*

Adding color to your wood

Staining & filling for character & camouflage

Even though a piece of furniture has been repaired and the surface smoothly sanded, it still might not be ready for the final finish. If you want your furniture to have a deep, clear, protective covering that shows off the natural wood grain, try adding some color to the surface before applying the final finishing coat.

Wood colors often change on their own as the wood ages, oxidizes, and reacts to light. Older furniture may already have a natural rich color or patina that you should be careful not to sand or bleach away during refinishing. Newer furniture, though, often has an attractive artificial patina that comes from the staining and filling of the wood during the piece's construction.

Always be aware that most wood fillers and stains are easily damaged by chemical finish removers; for this reason, once any part of the stain is gone, you must remove it all and renew it or the wood will appear blotchy and discolored under your clear final finish.

What staining can do

A good stain adds color to the wood and enhances the natural beauty of the grain. Many popular cabinet woods—such as mahogany, walnut, and other dark-colored woods—frequently need no additional stain. They often look their best with only the transparent oils and resins in a natural, clear finish.

On the other hand, most light-colored woods—including new pine, birch, fir, beech, ash, oak, and poplar—usually require some form of stain to give them more life and color. Aged pine, maple, and cherry, however, often already have a nice patina.

For the light woods, stain, followed by an adequate clear finishing coat, can be used by the refinisher in at least three ways:

• *Stain is excellent for giving light-colored woods more character than they usually have.* A golden oak stain, for example, goes a long way toward emphasizing the characteristic golden grain and open wood pores of fine oak. Even a few darker woods, such as Philippine mahogany and walnut, can often use some form of stain to further emphasize their deep grain patterns and to give them a warmer, richer appearance.

• *Stain is often used to give new wood an "aged" color.* Pine probably best illustrates this process—a pine stain on a new piece of unfinished pine furniture can add 100 years of artificial patina to the wood in about 15 minutes.

• *Stain may be used to make one type of wood look like another.* With the proper shade of stain, poplar, gum, and elm—all semi-hard, relatively plentiful cabinet woods with little, if any, natural color—can be made to look like mahogany, cherry, or walnut. Grain characteristics of the original wood and the stained imitation are different, of course, but it often takes a trained eye to detect this disguise.

WHICH STAIN DOES WHAT?

If you walk into a paint or hardware store to purchase wood stain, you'll be amazed at the many colors and kinds of stain that exist. Literally hundreds of possible color effects are possible, depending on the shade of stain you choose and the type of wood to which you apply it.

Many stain manufacturers attempt to help clear up this confusion by supplying color charts that are given away free to customers or are placed on display in the store. The tiny patches of color on these charts are intended to match the colors of the stains in the cans.

Though these color samples are often fairly accurate, you should rely on them only as a general guide to what your finished piece will look like. Be sure to test your stain in some out-of-the-way spot on your furniture before beginning to stain the whole piece.

Test stain on an out-of-the-way spot to check for proper color and density

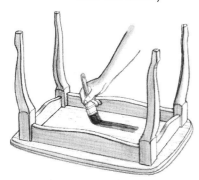

As recently as a few years ago, it was common for furniture finishers to mix their own stains from solvents and pigments. Mixing stains is still an interesting process and sometimes may be the only way to obtain a specific color. But with so many different types of wood stains available commercially, it seems logical for the refinishing novice to purchase a ready-made stain.

Various types of stains available include pigmented oil stains, penetrating oil stains, water stains, and non-grain-raising stains.

Pigmented oil stains are made of finely ground color pigments (similar to those used in coloring paints) mixed in a solution with tung oil, linseed oil, turpentine, or naphtha. This type of stain is really just a very thin paint; in fact, you can often make a good pigmented oil stain simply by thinning down any colored paint with turpentine.

Probably the most popular staining product for the home refinisher, pigmented oil stains can be purchased ready-mixed from any paint or hardware store under such names as "oil stains," "wood stains," "sealer stains," or possibly "pigmented wiping stains." All colors of this stain are nonfading and nonbleeding and are easy to apply with a brush or rag.

Unlike some other stains, pigmented oil stains use pigments instead of dyes to impart color to the wood. Because these pigments are opaque, they tend to conceal the grain pattern of the wood more completely than dyes do. Soft, porous woods darken a great deal when given a pigmented oil stain because they soak up more color; harder woods consistently absorb less.

For this reason, pigmented oil stains generally yield the best results on pine, fir, and all other softwoods, especially when one wood is being made to look like another. These stains also perform well on maple, birch, ash, and beech—all harder woods which take less stain. They are not good, though, when used on walnut, oak, mahogany, and similar hardwoods with open pores. The open pores in these woods often clog up with the finely ground color pigments, making the wood surface begin to look cloudy.

When using a pigmented oil stain, you must smoothly sand the wood first to ensure uniform stain penetration. Any cracks, dents, or scratches in the wood will catch more than their share of pigments, and the stain will only accentuate these surface irregularities. However, if you are attempting to simulate a "distressed" furniture finish (see Distressing Gives a Well-Aged Look, page 52), this unevenness may be just the effect you want.

Penetrating oil stains are often confused with pigmented oil stains on dealers' shelves. Though many products are labeled merely as "oil stains," pigmented stains can't really be considered true stains because they utilize solid pigments that add color by settling into the wood pores.

True penetrating oil stains, on the other hand, are composed of oil-soluble dyes, dissolved in a synthetic or natural oil-based liquid that penetrates the wood fibers to actually "stain" them with color.

Commonly known as colored "Danish oil," tung oil colored with analine dye, or colored "penetrating resin" (see Penetrating Resins, page 36), these stains have become very popular with wood finishers because they are easy to apply and they usually yield pleasing results. This finish (and it can honestly be called a "finish" because you rarely have to do anything else) is quite often clear with just a hint of color and can be used to build up a smooth, tough surface.

Because a penetrating oil uses no solid pigments, it is excellent for letting the natural beauty of the wood grain show through. This feature makes the stain especially attractive for use on such light-colored hardwoods as maple, cherry, birch, ash, and beech. It is also an excellent stain for darker woods—walnut and mahogany, for example.

Water stains are made from powdered analine dyes that dissolve in hot water and dye the fibers of the wood in the same way the fibers of a piece of cloth are dyed. These stains are inexpensive; the colors are clear, brilliant, warm-toned, and permanent. The penetration of a water stain into the wood surface is uniform even in woods of varying grains and densities, such as fir plywood. Use a water stain only on new wood, though—on previously stripped surfaces, you can expect uneven and blotchy penetration.

But all the advantages of a water stain can't be had without a few disadvantages, as well. Water stains swell the wood fibers and raise the grain, making light resanding necessary after you've lightly sealed the surface. If used excessively, a water stain may loosen glued joints, particularly on old pieces of furniture whose joints have not been reglued. Water stains also take longer to dry than other stains—at least 24 hours in some cases—and require a little extra care in application.

Some analine powders are labeled "water and alcohol-soluble," and these dyes may be dissolved in either water or wood alcohol or some of each. Though mixing a water stain in alcohol solves many of the inherent problems of water stains just mentioned, the stain is now even harder to apply because it dries so quickly.

Also, analine dyes do not produce the same color when mixed with alcohol as they do when mixed with water. Combined with water the dyes may yield a warm, reddish tone; but a cold, greenish stain will result if the powder is mixed in alcohol. If you like to experiment, you can obtain many interesting, colorful stains by varying the proportions of water and alcohol with dyes that are soluble in both.

Water stains are most effectively used on woods such as oak, cherry, or walnut that require only a slight boost in color to look more beautiful. If you have a hard time locating these stains in powdered form in your local paint or hardware store, you can easily order them by phone or through the catalogs of any large mail-order finishing supply firm.

Mix water stains according to instructions on the package—usually an ounce of dry powder to a quart of hot water—and add more water or stain to obtain either a lighter or darker color, according to your needs.

Water stains are now also being produced in ready-mixed form by some of the major stain manufacturers. Though not quite up to the quality of the traditional powdered version, the ready-mixed stains are easy to use, contain no flammable solvents, have no odor, and clean easily off hands and brushes with soap and water.

Non-grain-raising (NGR) stains, like water stains, use powdered analine dyes, but with an alcohol or petroleum by-product base that keeps the wood fibers from swelling. Non-grain-raising stains are usually more expensive than water stains because of the solvent used, but they have the advantage of being available in ready-mixed as well as powdered form.

The rapid drying of NGR stains makes application by brush difficult. However, smooth coats of stain are easily obtained with a spray gun (see page 72). The tones of NGR stains can always be controlled by thinning with the manufacturer's recommended thinner.

NGR stains are not suggested for use on pine, fir, spruce, or other softwoods; the wood's absorption rate would be uneven and the grain pattern would be too erratic. These stains are highly favored, though, for use on standard cabinet hardwoods, and they are the most commonly used stains in the furniture industry.

Because NGR stains are considered industrial products by most retailers, you will probably have difficulty finding them. Again, mail-order finishing supply firms are the answer.

If you purchase the stain in powder form, mix it according to the instructions on the package.

SUCCESSFUL STAINING TECHNIQUES

Stain is relatively easy to apply by a variety of methods, but most refinishers prefer to use a clean cloth or a brush (see Brushing and Spraying, page 69).

Try to keep the following staining tips in mind when you begin:

• *Surface preparation is the most important step* in the staining process. Since a stain always highlights the surface to which it is applied, be sure your piece has been thoroughly sanded first; then go over the surface one more time with medium steel wool to ensure uniform stain absorption (see Smoothing the Wood, page 20).

• *Always use a sealer on end grain;* this area is certain to over-absorb a stain (see Sealing the Surface, page 27). Softwoods and fir plywood should also be lightly sealed so that the uneven hardness of these woods will accept the stain more smoothly.

• *If you can't decide on the proper color,* start with a lighter rather than a darker stain. It is usually easy to add color to a lightly stained surface but very difficult to lighten a darker stain. Remember: Two coats of light stain are always better than one dark coat.

• *Begin by staining the least visible areas* of your furniture, always checking to make sure that the stain color, density, and absorption are what you had in mind. Your staining technique will get better as you progress.

• *Whenever possible, turn the piece as you work* so that you are always applying stain to a horizontal surface. When you must apply stain vertically, always start at the bottom of the piece and work upward. This method allows any sags or runs in the stain to be wiped up as you go and then blended into the rest of the stained surface.

• *If you make a mistake,* use a commercial bleach to remove the stain; then start over again (see Bleaching, page 26)—you'll have the advantage of recent practical experience to ensure a better job the second time around.

To apply a stain...

1. Brush or wipe stain onto wood surface

2. Then wipe excess stain off with a clean cloth in direction of wood grain

Apply pigmented stains according to the manufacturer's directions. If you plan on using more than one can of stain, mix all stain together in one large container first to ensure uniformity of stain color.

Pigmented oil stains should always be stirred well before they are used. Unlike dyes contained in other stains, the pigments in these oil stains settle to the bottom of the container during storage, and the stain must be remixed before (and during) use.

Let the stain dry 12 to 24 hours before applying the desired clear final finish.

Apply penetrating stains with a clean rag; then use the same rag to remove any oil surplus and to equalize the surface color. Wipe the stain while it is still wet, after allowing enough time to ensure good surface penetration. Make sure the last strokes with your rag are parallel to the wood grain. Wiping across the grain may leave streaks, especially if the stain is too dry.

Apply water stains to your furniture only after carefully experimenting with these dyes on a piece of scrap wood—preferably wood of the same type as your furniture. Since water stains usually dry lighter than the shade that first appears, let your test piece dry thoroughly before making any final color decisions.

To minimize raising of the wood grain when using a water stain, presponge the area to be stained with warm water; then lightly sand the surface before applying the stain. A water stain will dry in 12 to 24 hours.

Use a wash coat of 7 parts alcohol to 1 part shellac over the stain when it has dried (see Sealing the Surface, page 27). Then lightly sand the surface with 280-grit sandpaper to remove any remaining traces of raised grain.

Apply NGR stains with a spray gun (see Spray Gun Finishing, page 72). Because they are so quick to dry, these stains are difficult to apply with a brush. But if you must use a brush, first wash the work area quickly with NGR stain solvent; then immediately brush on full-strength stain. When using the brush method, work as quickly as possible and be careful to avoid lap marks, runs, and other forms of unevenness.

To fill or not to fill

As a tree grows, its trunk retains a large amount of water. This water is stored in the pores of the wood and lost when the tree is cut up for lumber and dried.

In oak, rosewood, mahogany, ash, walnut, teak, and other "open-grain" woods, the wood pores are large and very distinct. In "close-grain" woods, such as pine, cedar, fir, redwood, birch, and poplar, the pores are very small and barely noticeable—but still open. Many other woods have pores that fall between these two categories.

No matter how carefully you have sanded and stained your piece of furniture, the wood pores will still be open, and the wood surface will still be not completely smooth.

It may not matter to you whether the wood pores are left open or filled in. If you plan to give your furniture a penetrating finish (see Penetrating Resin, page 36) you'll probably want the pores to stay open—that's what gives this finish the natural, untouched look that makes it so popular. On the other hand, if you're refinishing an antique mahogany dining table, you'll undoubtedly want the deep, glasslike surface that comes only from using a wood filler before the final finishing coat.

If you plan on applying a light-colored stain to your furniture, apply the filler first, lightly sand when dry, and follow with either a pigmented or penetrating oil stain. If a darker stain is desired, apply the stain first and follow it with a filler tinted darker than the stain with ordinary paint tinting colors. All fillers dry lighter than they appear when applied.

SELECTING THE RIGHT FILLER

Wood filler is used to fill the pores of wood in order to provide a flat surface for finishing. Fillers can be purchased in two forms: paste and liquid.

Paste fillers—for use on open-grain woods—can be purchased in either semitransparent or opaque forms; liquid fillers used on close-grain woods are usually transparent. It is always a good idea to use a wood filler that is as transparent as possible so the filler won't hide the wood's natural color and beauty.

Filler may also be mixed with wood stain so that staining and filling can both be done at once. Some paint and hardware dealers sell a type of ready-mixed filler stain for just this purpose, and when the product is used properly according to the manufacturer's directions, the results are quite satisfactory.

If you prefer to make your own stain/filler combination, mix the filler of your choice with any commonly available pigmented oil stain.

Paste filler is the most commonly used type of wood filler. It has a pastelike consistency (much like that of peanut butter) which usually must be thinned before it is ready to use. This type of filler is most often suitable for such open-grain woods as oak, mahogany, and walnut.

The best fillers available to the home refinisher are known as sanding fillers and usually have a ground silicate base. Sanding fillers have several advantages. They fill the pores in one application, dry transparent, do not change the wood color, can be colored, and can be sanded to a very smooth finish. You may have to shop around and read the labels to find these fillers.

Many paint and hardware stores carry fillers with a cornstarch base. They are quite good but may require several applications to fill the wood pores completely.

Fillers are usually purchased in a light creamy gray or "natural" color and then mixed, according to the manufacturer's directions, with small amounts of oil stain or paint tinting colors to obtain the final desired shade. It is usually a good idea to mix the filler a little darker than the stained wood itself to help emphasize the wood's grain pattern and beauty.

Liquid filler is really nothing more than a thin sanding sealer containing a very small quantity of solids. These solids fill the wood pores in the same manner as a paste filler, but because liquid fillers are so thin, they are useful only on fine-grain woods. Some wood finishers find a liquid filler useful on maple, birch, poplar, and cherry; many other finishers don't bother with this extra step on these same woods.

Ordinary shellac makes a good liquid filler. White shellac is best for natural and light-colored finishes, orange shellac for the darker finishes. To use shellac as a filler, thin it with denatured alcohol to obtain a 2-pound cut (see The Classic Look of Shellac, page 38). Apply two coats of this mixture, sanding lightly between applications.

HOW TO APPLY FILLERS

Before using any paste filler, be sure it is thinned (according to the manufacturer's directions) to the desired working consistency. Turpentine or paint thinner (mineral spirits) are standard thinning agents. The amount of thinning, though, depends on the size of the wood pores to be filled.

Whichever paste filler you choose, apply it liberally with a brush on only a small area of your project at a time. Remember to stir a paste filler continually during use. If all the pigments settle to the bottom of the can, the filling properties of a paste filler will be greatly reduced.

Allow the filler to set for 10 to 20 minutes; then wipe vigorously across the wood grain with a piece of burlap or other coarse cloth. This brisk wiping pushes the paste filler well down into the wood pores and also removes the excess. Finally, lightly wipe the wood surface in the direction of the grain.

Let the paste filler dry for at least 24 hours; then sand the surface lightly in the direction of the grain to remove any filler that may be lying above the pores. Be sure to remove all surplus filler during this step—any filler left behind may cause a streaked or cloudy effect in the final finish.

A last wash coat of thin shellac is always good insurance to prevent any paste filler from bleeding through to the finishing coat.

Liquid fillers are simply brushed on the wood surface like any regular finish—there is no need to rub the filler into the grain. When the wood pores are not large, the application of several thin coats of liquid filler combined with careful sanding between coats is all that's needed to achieve a smooth surface.

...Using filler

1. Filling *open-pored wood is easy. Begin by brushing filler vigorously onto wood in direction of grain.*

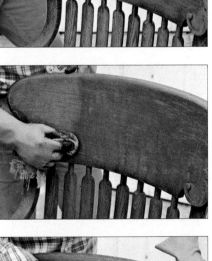

2. With same brush, *brush paste filler across grain, working filler deep into open pores.*

3. With a rag, *wipe filler off across grain, further pushing filler down deeply as possible into pores.*

4. Finally, wipe filler *off one last time in direction of grain. This should remove all excess.*

Choosing a finish *may not always be as clear cut as it might seem.*

Apply penetrating resin *by pouring it on surface and wiping it evenly around with rag. By soaking into wood, the penetrating resin will provide some protection for wood pores.*

Polyurethane finishes *are available in two surface lusters. Gloss polyurethane was used for fern stand, satin polyurethane for oak chair. If you decide to fill open-grain wood such as oak, choose a filler compatible with urethanes.*

Choosing the final wood finish

The most popular finishes— their selection & use

Good furniture finishes protect and beautify wood surfaces. Clear finishes are especially popular because they emphasize and enhance the charm of natural wood color and grain. Of course, clear finishes require more careful surface preparation than paints do. But once your project has been properly sanded and stained (or otherwise cleaned and prepared for painting) you are ready to select a final protective coating.

Today, any trip to the paint or hardware store will reveal a wide variety of wood finishing products. And new chemical developments add to that variety.

One of these new developments is a line of coatings and paints that clean up with water, have the advantages of petroleum solvent-based finishes, but with significantly less solvents. The unpleasant smell and harmful effects of solvent fumes are virtually eliminated.

The material that follows will help you select an appropriate finishing product as will the staff of the paint or hardware store.

Simple finishing choices

It will simplify your finishing choice to know that all furniture finishing products generally fall into one of two basic types: penetrating finishes or surface coatings. Other wood finishes are often only variations of these.

Penetrating finishes soak into the wood pores to give a natural, "no-finish" look and feel to all furniture surfaces. Though a penetrating finish sinks into the wood and hardens below the wood surface, it is still surprisingly durable and can often resist abrasion, stains, chemicals, and liquids without the glasslike look of a more protective coating.

Natural and synthetic oils and resins are the most popular penetrating finishes. The natural ones—linseed oil and lemon oil— have played a major role in traditional furniture finishing. Today, however, the more modern Danish oils, penetrating resins, and other synthetic "plastic" finishes

are far more popular because they are equally as beautiful as natural oil—and easier to use.

Surface coatings lie on the surface of the wood and provide protection in the form of a thin, durable furniture shield. This protective covering is often glasslike in appearance but can be dulled down to a low-gloss sheen whenever necessary by a number of different methods. When properly maintained, a good surface finish will make your furniture relatively safe from dropped objects, scratches, stains, chemicals, heat, and other potential finish destroyers.

One type of surface finish is shellac, which mixes readily with alcohol and dries on the surface of the wood as the alcohol evaporates. When repairs to the finish are needed, it's easy to apply more alcohol to make the shellac redissolve and then dry again as before. Of course, this could also be a disadvantage—spill a cocktail on a shellac finish and your surface protection is likely to disappear.

Another type of surface finish is lacquer, which is very similar to shellac, except that it is harder and more durable. Even with these advantages, though, lacquer is infrequently used by the do-it-yourself finisher because it dries so quickly and is difficult to apply successfully without spray equipment (see Brushing & Spraying, page 69). Special

brushing lacquers can be purchased, however; these are explained on page 45.

Varnish is an excellent choice for a durable surface finish. Traditional varnishes were originally developed when linseed oil and shellac were mixed together. The shellac dried the linseed oil; in return, the linseed oil made the shellac resistant to alcohol and water. Many modern synthetic finishes, as well as "plastic" varnishes (polyurethanes) and various paints and enamels, are

now merely offshoots of this original varnish-type base.

For each type of wood finish available on the market today, there is a furniture finisher somewhere who swears by it and who wouldn't use anything else. The best finish for you depends on your particular project, your experience, and whether your final finishing goal is appearance, durability, ease of application, or ease of maintenance—or all four (see What to Look For in a New Finish, page 7).

Easy-to-use synthetics

Not long ago, furniture finishers considered synthetic finishes to be different from other varnishes, paints, and lacquers. Today, nearly all varnishes, paints, and lacquers *are* synthetics.

The term "synthetics" is now commonly used in the wood finishing industry to describe finishing products mixed with manmade or synthetic oils and resins, compared to those products made with oils and resins dug from the ground or gathered from a plant or a tree.

Modern chemistry is rapidly advancing the art of wood finishing by supplying increasingly better synthetics in the furniture finishes available to consumers. All major finishing manufacturers sponsor research and development laboratories where new chemicals are developed and existing products are reassessed.

A clear synthetic finish is now the most popular wood coating in use by the do-it-yourself finisher. Though not inexpensive, synthetics are in great demand because they are heat, chemical, water, and scuff resistant, as well as being easy to apply and available everywhere. The most useful synthetic finishes are sold under these names: penetrating resins, catalytic sealers, and polyurethane varnishes.

PENETRATING RESINS

A penetrating resin finish—often called "penetrating wood sealer,"

"Danish oil," or even "plastic oil sealer"—is the most popular oil finish in use today. Easy to apply and maintain, a penetrating resin gives wood a durable finish that resists alcohol, heat, household chemicals, water, and most minor scratches.

If you're looking for a protective finish that lets you enjoy the natural texture and "feel" of the open wood grain, a penetrating resin is the right finish for you. Use penetrating resin finishes over stain or purchase them in premixed, wood-tone colors to add a slightly dark wood shading wherever needed.

All penetrating finishes soak into the pores of the wood, filling the cells with a synthetic or plasticlike material that hardens in the surface fibers. When dry, wood treated with a penetrating finish is measurably harder and slightly darker—an effect that greatly enhances the grain pattern and color of the wood surface.

Choose a penetrating resin for any piece of furniture that you don't want to have the "wood-under-glass" look of an on-the-surface finish. Penetrating finishes have probably gained widest acceptance on modern Scandinavian-style furniture; for such pieces, the more natural and finish-free a wood can look, the better. These finishes are equally popular for antiques, on which penetrating finishes show off the fine old woods to best advantage.

The most interesting finishing

results with a penetrating resin are obtained on hard, open-grain woods, such as oak, teak, or walnut, that have been well sanded and left free of wood filler. When a penetrating resin finish is used on close-grain woods, such as pine and fir, the results are less satisfactory.

Ease of application makes penetrating finishes perfect for use both on large pieces of furniture and on intricate surfaces. Penetrating resins are also highly suitable for finishing wood paneling; they are probably most extensively used on wood floors. Some brands of resins are primarily intended for wood flooring, but you will find these varieties especially rugged and useful for furniture too. Penetrating resins are not meant to be used on outdoor furniture.

Apply penetrating resin to an inconspicuous part of the furniture (or to a matching piece of scrap wood) first as a test before you begin to finish the entire surface.

If the sample color and texture are what you had in mind, proceed to liberally apply the resin to the wood with a brush or rag. Work on a horizontal surface whenever possible. Don't worry about brush marks during application; the finish will even out as it dries. Many furniture finishers don't use a brush but simply pour the finish directly from the can onto the wood; then they spread the resin around with a rag or with a pad of very fine (4/0) steel wool.

Allow the surface to stay wet

for half an hour or longer, depending on the manufacturer's instructions. If the surface begins to dull, this indicates that all the liquid has soaked into the wood and you should apply more resin to keep the surface wet.

When the wood has absorbed all the resin you think it will take, use clean rags to wipe off the remaining surface liquid.

A second—even a third—application of resin is usually a good idea, especially if the wood is very porous. Wait 24 hours between resin coats. You'll know when it's time to stop—when the wood won't accept any more of the finish. The more resin absorbed by the wood, the tougher the finish coating and the harder the finished surface.

If the surface of your furniture is later scratched or marred, just apply more penetrating resin to the damaged area with fine steel wool. The surface scratches will absorb the resin and the new finish will blend in with the color of the original one.

CATALYTIC SEALERS

Catalytic sealer finishes—often called "liquid plastics" or various other names—are synthetic finishes that cure on the wood with a catalytic or hardening agent that you add to the finish just before you apply it. Since the amount of catalyst varies from one product to another, be sure to check manufacturer's directions for the one you've selected. Catalytic sealers usually take from 1 to 4 hours to dry to a rock-hard finish.

The major advantage of a catalytic sealer is the hard, tough coating it produces, making this finish one of the most durable around. This type of finish transforms the wood surface into a virtual sheet of plastic that is impervious to moisture, alcohol, chemicals, and burns.

Choose a catalytic sealer for any surface where you want a thick, clear protective finishing coat—bar tops, game tables, children's toys, and small, decorative découpage pieces (see Creative? Try Découpage, page 61).

Since the introduction of the penetrating resins and synthetic varnishes (polyurethanes) that give a more "natural" look to wood, catalytic resin finishes have lost some of their popularity. But even though they are not as convenient to use as the other synthetics, catalytic sealers are excellent finishes to achieve that deep, glossy, "wood-under-glass" look of liquid plastic.

Apply a catalytic sealer immediately after mixing it with the hardening agent according to the manufacturer's directions. Use this finish only over unfinished or lightly stained wood, since any kind of wood sealer or heavily pigmented stain is likely to cause poor adhesion of a resin finish.

Catalytic finishes may be sprayed, brushed, or even poured onto the wood surface. They usually dry hard enough to be sanded in 1 to 4 hours. If you apply a second coat, it should dry at least 24 hours before the final smoothing. Rub the dried surface with a rubbing compound or with extra-fine, waterproof sandpaper (see Rubbing & Waxing, pages 48-49) and rubbing oil or water for that special, deep gloss shine.

Some catalytic finishes require baking under high heat to cure properly. The baking equipment doesn't have to be elaborate—one or two infrared heat lamps are all you need for excellent results.

POLYURETHANE FINISHES

Polyurethane finishes are among the most popular furniture finishing products. Except for a few brands of spar varnishes for use on boats and the occasional cabinet varnish that requires a great deal of rubbing by hand, natural-resin varnishes are rare.

Today, 75 percent of all varnishes produced contain such manmade resins as acrylic, phenolic, alkyd, urethane, and vinyl. These synthetic varnishes often go on more easily, last longer, and offer more surface protection than their old-fashioned natural resin counterparts.

Because polyurethanes are sometimes referred to as "varnishes" even though they have a synthetic composition, complete instructions on when, where, and how to use these modern finishes are included in the section called Varnish—Durable and Protective, page 43.

Oil for a natural finish

Oils are available in many varieties and for many purposes, ranging from automobile engine oil to oil for squeaking door hinges. The only oils that concern a furniture finisher, though, are the ones available from paint and hardware dealers for use on wood surfaces. Listed in order of popularity and usefulness, these products are Danish, linseed, and lemon oil.

DANISH OIL

The term "Danish oil" was first used to identify the predominantly clear finish found on Scandinavian furniture. This synthetic oil (not to be confused with a natural petroleum-based oil, such as linseed oil or lemon oil) is virtually the same as products labeled "penetrating resin."

Like a penetrating resin, Danish oil flows onto the wood surface and soaks into the wood pores, hardening there and leaving a natural, no-finish look. You apply Danish oil as you would any penetrating finish—directions are on page 36.

A good Danish oil finish is so highly superior to the traditional boiled linseed oil finish that it should be the only oil finish applied by the beginning finisher.

BOILED LINSEED OIL

Not to be confused with *raw* linseed oil is *boiled* linseed oil, whose use as a penetrating finish is rooted in furniture finishing tradition. Some dyed-in-the-wool furniture craftsmen still feel there is no finer finish to be found than boiled linseed oil, and this natural oil's effect on antique wood surfaces has often been praised. The truth of the matter is, though, that applying boiled linseed oil can take a very long time.

Although linseed is now far less popular than either Danish oil or penetrating resin, if you decide to try this classic finishing product you will find boiled linseed oil to be fairly resistant to heat, alcohol, and water—but only after many successive layers have been applied.

Mix the straight boiled linseed oil with an equal amount of turpentine or mineral spirits to aid in application and drying. Brush this mixture sparingly onto the wood and allow enough time for adequate penetration (until the newly wetted surface loses its gloss). When the wood pores and grain have absorbed all the oil they can hold, wipe the surface briskly with a clean, dry cloth.

Once you have started this procedure, repeat it several times during the first day; then repeat once a day for a week, once a week for a month, and once a month for the life of the furniture. After you feel that the "world's slowest finish" looks as beautiful as you had intended it to, wax or polish the surface for final protection. If you don't protect the oil in some way, you'll be unable to remove the dust that builds up on the surface. Remove the wax with paint thinner every so often to avoid a waxy buildup.

There is a much quicker way to achieve nearly the same patina for a boiled linseed oil finish. Try to alternate applications of the oil and a good penetrating resin. Oil as a first coat enhances the color of the wood; penetrating resin as a second coat protects the first coat of oil; finally, oil as a third coat gives the wood surface the pleasant odor and natural feel of an old-fashioned, hand-rubbed finish.

LEMON OIL

If not overused, lemon oil is a good product. It is excellent for cleaning and protecting fine woods, but don't consider lemon oil alone a final finish. It's better used over final finishes to "feed" the wood, replacing the natural wood oils as they evaporate. If these oils are not replaced, wood often becomes dry and brittle and absorbs moisture from the air. Moisture will expand dry wood, and, over a period of time, this shrinking and expanding may cause cracks and checks on the wood surface and can loosen glued furniture joints.

The classic look of shellac

Long the standard by which all other finishes have been judged, shellac is certainly one of the most beautiful wood coatings available to the beginning finisher. Shellac's versatility and unique characteristics put it in a class by itself.

Shellac has many disadvantages, though, which have caused its popularity to decrease in proportion to the rapid rise of the modern synthetics. Shellac can be dissolved in alcohol—that includes spilled nail polish and cocktails—as well as in ammonia, strong soaps and detergents, and even hard water. For this reason, furniture finished with shellac usually has to be frequently retouched.

This constant retouching makes shellac unsuitable for finishing table tops and other vulnerable areas where accidents are likely to happen. On the other hand, when used as a finish for chairs, picture frames, decorative wooden items, and other objects, shellac offers a quick, clear, fast-drying (dust-free in 30 minutes), beautiful, glossy finish.

The disadvantages of shellac become advantages when repairs need to be made to the finish. Because shellac is soluble in denatured alcohol, most surface scratches, abrasions, and blemishes can usually be repaired by the process of reamalgamation (see page 66).

Shellac is at its best on the darker cabinet woods. Its qualities of superb adhesion, flexibility, brilliance, and abrasion resistance have kept shellac available on paint dealers' shelves despite the overwhelming popularity of modern synthetics. Shellac is still the most popular finish for French polishing (see page 40).

For use as a sanding, staining or filling sealer (see page 27), shellac is the traditional choice—many good furniture finishers always brush on a light coat of shellac first, even if they plan to use a more durable varnish later. Never use a polyurethane varnish over shellac, though, because adhesion is generally very poor.

HOW TO BUY SHELLAC

Shellac should always be bought fresh and in a small enough quantity for just the immediate project. Because shellac deteriorates if it sits too long on a dealer's shelf, you should select your shellac in a store with enough turnover to assure continually fresh stock. When in doubt as to the quality of shellac, be sure to test it first on a piece of scrap wood. Shellac that dries on the test piece with a tacky surface is too old and will remain tacky if used on your furniture.

The do-it-yourself finisher who shops for shellac will often find both white and orange shellac available. "Water white" shellac is intended for light finishes, and orange shellac is suitable for browns and mahoganies. The amber cast of the orange shellac is especially effective on walnut and mahogany.

Shellac is sold in "cuts." A "4-pound cut" means that 4 pounds of dry shellac flakes have been dissolved in 1 gallon of denatured alcohol. To make a 1-pound cut from a 4-pound cut (the most commonly available), simply add 3 parts of denatured alcohol to 1 part of the shellac you have already purchased. Use these same proportions to adjust for lesser amounts. It makes no difference which cut you happen to buy, since you'll thin the shellac before use anyway.

When mixing shellac, it is not important for your measurements to be exact. You will soon learn by

(Continued on page 42)

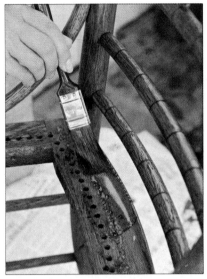

Shellac *is traditional finish for antique mahogany sewing table and oak side chair.*

1. Apply shellac *as you would any other clear finish—with clean brush on clean wood surface. If your first coat is thin, later coats will be easier to apply.*

2. Sand shellac *between coats with fine abrasive paper or steel wool. Since shellac is multiple-coat finish, each coat should adhere well to the next.*

3. Apply second coat *to wood immediately after sanding. Shellac dries so quickly that 4 or 5 coats can be applied in less than a day.*

french polish

The luxury of a French polish finish—thin, multiple coats of shellac—has traditionally been found on only the most expensive and cherished antiques. Long favored for use on Louis XIV, Chippendale, Sheraton, and Hepplewhite furniture, French polish was used not only for its beauty but also for its practicality. No other finish can equal its tough, velvety sheen. And no other finish can be as easily repaired if accidentally damaged.

Since any fine French polish finish requires a fair amount of time and energy, it's usually not practical for today's commercially made furniture. But for the home wood finisher who wants to refinish a beautiful antique, or the one who has already spent hundreds of hours making something from scratch in the garage, the extra time that French polishing takes is well worth the effort. French polish will give the wood a smooth, thin finish—full of luster, but without the thick, high gloss of varnish or polyurethane.

If the wood in your chosen project needs staining before finishing, use only water-base aniline dye stains. Other types may lift during the extensive rubbing process. As with all other finishing procedures, practicing on a small scrap of wood before you begin on a cherished antique will lead more surely to a beautiful, trouble-free final project.

Peeking into places *they're not supposed to be is great fun for children. With its shiny French polish finish, this antique music box looks brand new.*

1. Make French polishing pad *by forming wad of gauze, cotton, or cheesecloth into small ball for conical-shaped core. Then, lightly wrap core with piece of lint-free cotton or linen. Cut and fold cloth so it's just large enough to fit your hand comfortably.*

2. Squeeze pad against palm *after you dip pad lightly in boiled linseed oil and then in 4-lb. cut of shellac (see page 38); squeezing motion mixes two finishes together. Make sure face of pad is free of wrinkles so that finish will be smoothly applied to wood.*

3. Pad shellac/oil mixture *gently onto wood with rocking motion of your wrist. Work quickly to cover entire area, being careful to blend each padding stroke in with the next. Repeat shellac/oil applications, trying to work finish deeply into surface.*

4. Apply rubbing oil and pumice *or rottenstone (see page 49) to dry shellac/oil surface. If you use cork sanding block wrapped with clean rag, final surface should be flawless, with deep lustre, and will only need coat of wax to ensure final protection.*

. . . Continued from page 38

experience that about one part shellac for every two parts alcohol will be about right. The thinner the shellac, the more easily it can be applied and the faster it dries.

THE TECHNIQUE OF APPLYING SHELLAC

Shellac is definitely not a one coat finish. You must build a finish with two, three, or more coats before you can begin to enjoy the luster on the wood. But because shellac dries dust-free in 15 to 30 minutes and is recoatable in 2 to 4 hours (depending on humidity, penetration, and shellac consistency), an entire final finish of shellac takes only a day or so to complete.

Also, since the solvents in liquid shellac soften dry shellac surfaces, you can go back to repair any mistakes you made in the preceding coat. Perfect blending and adhesion of overlapped and successive coats of shellac are virtually guaranteed.

If you have never worked with shellac before, begin with a 1-pound cut—it is thinner and more forgiving of mistakes. Begin by brushing on a full, wet coat of shellac with a slow, smooth motion. Take special care to overlap all adjoining brush strokes and to develop a clean, smooth surface.

After about 2 hours, when the first coat of shellac is dry, rub or sand the high spots off with 4/0-grade steel wool or 320-grit open-coat abrasive paper. Apply a second coat of shellac the same way as you did the first; when it, too, is dry, rub it down as you did before.

The third coat should be smooth enough for final rubbing. If not, rub or sand the surface down one last time and apply more shellac. To obtain a flat, waxable surface, use 4/0 steel wool and rubbing oil (see Rubbing & Waxing, page 48) to rub out any glassy or shiny spots.

If a classic high gloss shellac finish is what you want, allow at least 3 days for the new finish to harden properly; then follow the pumice and rottenstone rubbing methods detailed on page 48. A hard paste wax can be applied 24 hours after the last surface treatment is completed.

...Using a polyurethane finish

1. Use modern polyurethane *finish on any wood where you need maximum surface protection.*

2. Sand *between first and second coats for good mechanical bond. 180-grit abrasive is recommended.*

3. Apply second coat *if necessary for added protection. Polyurethane is thick finish, dries rock-hard.*

Optional step: *apply paste wax to dry surface for extra protection from scratches.*

Varnish-durable and protective

Varnish is probably the toughest, most water and heat-resistant finish you can choose for your wood. Even though a good modern varnish (polyurethane) takes longer to apply and to dry than shellac, varnish is so much more durable that it is usually the first finishing choice among home woodworkers.

Most varnishes are available in "glossy," "satin," or "flat" finishes. Glossy varnish has a high shine to it that simulates a striking, hand-rubbed finish. If a glossy shine doesn't appeal to you, use steel wool or wet sandpaper to rub down the finish when it has dried.

Better yet, save yourself the trouble and extra work of dulling a glossy finish by using varnish labeled "satin" or "flat." These finishes are less shiny and give the wood a semiglossy or flat look when dry.

THE MODERN VARNISH FINISH

Not many years ago, all varnishes were made by mixing different proportions of natural resins with linseed oils and turpentine. Each different resin-oil formula had a different name—piano varnish, gymnasium varnish, bar top varnish, and so on—to correspond with the way it was used.

The more oil used in a varnish, the less brittle and more durable the varnish would be. These were called "long oil" varnishes. But too much linseed oil in the mixture caused problems with finish hardness and took too long to dry.

Varnishes with less oil—or "short oil" varnishes—dried much harder and the finish could be sanded between coats. A short oil varnish was excellent for a beautiful hand-rubbed finish, but it was brittle and scratched easily, and it often cracked rather quickly on the surface. In short, choosing the right varnish for a particular need used to be no easy feat.

Today, natural-resin varnishes are nearly a thing of the past. A few long-oil spar varnishes are still available for use on boats, and natural-resin varnishes can still be purchased, but the majority of all varnishes now contain the newer synthetic resins. These resins make varnishes easier to apply, longer lasting, and faster drying. Synthetics also produce a better surface finish than any of the previous oil-resin varnish combinations.

The resins used most in today's varnishes are alkyd, phenolic, and polyurethane. Alkyd resins, usually the least expensive, are used primarily in colored varnishes and economy brands. Phenolic resins are found in exterior varnishes and in some of the special clear varnishes for use on boats. Polyurethanes are the most popular and most expensive resins. However, many wood finishers feel the cost of polyurethanes is justified because their ability to hold up under heat, chemicals, and abuse is the greatest of all the synthetic varnishes.

Other synthetic resins are also available in special varnishes for special jobs. These include epoxy, silicone, acrylic, vinyl, and water emulsion-based varnishes. Since the world of synthetic finishes is constantly changing, it is always best to check with your paint dealer about new products and their specific intended uses.

WAYS TO AVOID VARNISHING PROBLEMS

Varnish has traditionally been a difficult finish to apply. Thanks to recent chemical developments and the universal use of synthetics, though, this job is now much easier. To avoid specific varnishing problems, you should be aware of how some of these problems occur.

Dust is probably the worst enemy of varnish. A modern varnish finish takes from 2 to 6 hours to dry, and for that entire time the surface is susceptible to dust. Always try to work in the most dust-free area you can find—an empty guest room, for example, is an ideal choice. If you have no choice but to varnish your piece in the garage, be sure to clean the interior of the garage thoroughly before you begin to work.

Place the furniture to be varnished in the location you've chosen and clean the piece thoroughly with a vacuum cleaner or sticky tack rag (available at any paint or hardware store). Then leave the room for 3 or 4 hours to let the dust settle before you begin varnishing.

Clothes can carry dust, too. Clean clothes made of synthetic materials are much better to wear than wool when applying a varnish finish. But whatever you wear, complete the job quickly and try not to move around too much in the process.

Runs can be avoided if you always do your varnishing on a horizontal surface. Remove drawers, doors, and anything else that can be laid flat before you start to work. And don't load your brush with too much varnish at any one time—it will only drip from the bristles when you least expect it.

Dry spots in the varnish can be caught before you finish working if you place your furniture facing a window or light. Positioning the piece in this manner creates a reflection from the newly wet wood surface that will let you constantly check for brush marks, dry spots, and drips.

Clouds in the finish may result from your brush if it has been used previously for painting. Whenever possible, try to set aside one special brush to use only for varnishing. If you don't have a special brush set aside and you doubt the cleanliness of the brushes you do have, it is worthwhile to buy a new brush.

Clouds can also result if a modern polyurethane varnish is applied over a previous shellac finish—the solvents used in the two products are not usually compatible.

Bubbles that remain on the newly finished surface are a nuisance. As the varnish dries, the bubbles break, causing little pin holes or craters that are hard to remove.

Bubbles can come from a number of sources. For instance, varnish should never be shaken before use—always stir it slowly and thoroughly and allow it to stand until the air bubbles in the liquid disappear. Bubbles can also result if you drag the brush bristles over the lip of the varnish can before you begin to brush. Instead, always tap the brush tip gently against the inside of the can to remove any extra liquid.

All varnishing should be a smooth operation with only the minimum amount of air allowed to mix with the varnish finish.

SUCCESSFUL VARNISHING TECHNIQUES

Take your time when applying a protective coat of varnish. The wood surface should shine through the varnish, and the more wood grain visible, the better. Therefore all the wood must be prepared as carefully as possible before you apply the first finishing coat. Here are preparation steps for three different conditions:

• *Before varnishing over bare wood,* examine the surface thoroughly for sandpaper marks, dirt, dust, and oily fingerprints. If necessary, clean the surface with mineral spirits (paint thinner) or lacquer thinner. If more sanding is needed, go over the entire surface with the finest grit sandpaper and then go over it again with fine steel wool. This method will open the wood pores to allow for equal varnish penetration.

• *Before varnishing over stained wood,* be sure the stain has had adequate time to dry. Test the varnish in some inconspicuous spot first to determine if the final shade is what you had in mind. If the color isn't just right, you can darken it slightly with a second application of a more diluted stain or lighten it by rapid rubbing with your particular stain's solvent (see page 30).

• *Before varnishing over an old finish,* make sure the previous finish is adhering well to the wood and is absolutely clean. To achieve the best possible adhesion, wash the old finish with detergent and water or rub it with a little paint thinner (mineral spirits) or alcohol and fine steel wool. If much of the old finish is still glossy, scratch it lightly with fine sandpaper to roughen it so the new finish will adhere.

• *Before varnishing over filled wood,* first be sure that the filler is thoroughly dry. Some varnishing solvents occasionally will react unfavorably with the various solvents found in fillers. So, if the filler is not completely dry (or has not been adequately sealed—see page 27), you may find that it will "bleed" through into the final finish, spoiling it. Whenever in doubt, always test the varnish first on the filled surface.

• *Before varnishing a second or third coat* over a previous varnish finish, carefully scuff sand all the in-between coats first. Why is it important to insure a good mechanical bond before you begin? Because many of the more modern polyurethane varnishes don't really adhere very well to one another, and their solvents won't melt the solvents on the previous finishing level to form a good chemical bond.

Apply varnish straight from the can, if you like. However, if you want your first varnish coat to act as a sealer coat, try diluting some of the varnish with the thinner recommended on the label. A thin first coat of varnish always makes

For applying varnish...

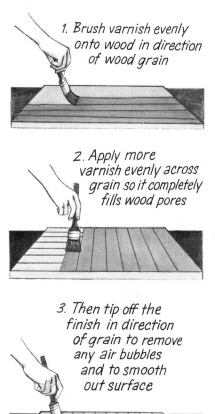

1. Brush varnish evenly onto wood in direction of wood grain

2. Apply more varnish evenly across grain so it completely fills wood pores

3. Then tip off the finish in direction of grain to remove any air bubbles and to smooth out surface

an excellent base for subsequent heavier coats.

Begin by dipping your brush in the varnish almost halfway up the bristles, touching off the extra varnish on the inside of the can. Apply the varnish liberally to the wood with long, smooth continuous strokes.

After you apply the varnish parallel to the wood grain, quickly cross-stroke with your brush at right angles across the grain. Complete the process by stroking lightly along the grain again, this time using only the tips of the bristles. This procedure is often referred to as the "tick-tack-toe" varnishing technique, and it effectively works the finish deep into the open wood pores.

Because varnish dries so slowly compared with shellac and lacquer, you'll have plenty of time to work. Use the least number of brush strokes you can and work in one small section at a time—don't try to do the whole piece of furniture at once. If your brush loses a bristle in the varnished surface, try removing it by carefully poking at the bristle with the wet tip of the brush to pick it up.

Analyze the finish after your varnish begins to cover the surface. Go back and check where each "tick-tack-toe" section joins the next. If the joining areas show any lap marks that won't level out, the overlapped edges are beginning to dry too soon because your sections have been too large. Learn from your experience and brush the finish over a smaller area next time.

If too many lap marks appear or if something else goes wrong with your initial varnishing, remedy all problems in the next finishing coat. With practice, you'll soon learn just how large an area you can cover successfully with minimum effort and maximum finishing results.

When you've finished varnishing and analyzing, leave the room and stay away for at least 24 hours. If the weather is damp, plan on staying away from your newly varnished piece at least twice as long as usual. And always read the manufacturer's instructions on the varnish label for specific drying time.

Sand your furniture between coats of varnish to remove the gloss and to provide a good surface for the next coat to adhere to. Use 400-grit wet or dry sandpaper and be careful not to sand completely through the previous finish, especially on edges and trim.

Two coats of a good, clear varnish will usually result in an excellent surface. One coat will be sufficient for picture frames or for furniture that receives only light use. But to obtain the finest and hardest finish, it is a good idea to apply three or four coats of varnish, carefully sanding between each additional application.

After the final coat is completely dry you can lightly rub the surface with fine steel wool (4/0) for a satin finish. For a distinctive high gloss, use either pumice and oil or rottenstone and oil (see Rubbing & Waxing, pages 48-49).

Lacquer-fast, dust-free drying

Modern lacquer is a fast-drying synthetic finish similar to shellac—but without some of shellac's disadvantages. Lacquer is much more tolerant of heat, alcohol, and moisture than shellac is, and it dries dust-free much faster than varnish. Properly applied, lacquer is the thinnest of all surface finishes.

For the do-it-yourself finisher and refinisher, though, lacquer is much less useful than either shellac or varnish because it is often difficult to apply. A principal ingredient of lacquer is acetone, which is more volatile than alcohol and evaporates almost instantly, causing the lacquer to dry almost instantly. The best lacquers are sprayed on furniture and are dry to the touch in 10 seconds. Brushing lacquers are now available that dry more slowly, but even these lacquers require careful application.

SPRAY LACQUER—OR BRUSH IT

The major difference between "spraying lacquer" and "brushing lacquer" is drying time. Don't ever attempt to brush a spraying lacquer—it will dry before adequately covering the surface. If you want to spray a brushing lacquer, though, it's easy to do, and the results are usually excellent.

Spraying lacquers were originally developed for use on furniture production lines. The rapid drying time and easy application of this finish made it perfect for use in furniture factories and other high volume woodworking firms.

To use spraying lacquers in your own home, you'll need a spray gun with air compressor and motor, as well as a well-ventilated area in which to spray. A spray apparatus is not a bad investment if you plan to do much finishing work. The same equipment can be used to spray shellac, varnish, and paint (see Spray Gun Finishing, page 72)—it can even inflate your auto tires.

Spraying lacquers are also available in aerosol cans. Though spray cans are often expensive and inefficient for large-scale work, they are fine for small projects. Sprays are especially useful for building up a multilayer finish because they leave no brush strokes.

Brushing lacquers, now readily available in most paint or hardware stores, produce one of the best glossy finishes around. The advantages of brushing lacquers are twofold: such rapid drying time that they hardly collect any dust, and excellent resistance to water and alcohol.

Various disadvantages of brushing lacquers center around their quick-drying solvents, which force some stains and wood fillers to bleed through the finish if they haven't been properly sealed. Also, brushing lacquer often dries very quickly, making it difficult for the do-it-yourself finisher to apply.

TIPS FOR SUCCESSFUL LACQUERING

Brushing a lacquer onto a wood surface is similar to using varnish except that the lacquer will dry much faster. For best results, always thin lacquer first according to the manufacturer's instructions and never work with lacquer that won't flow easily onto your furniture. If you've used a pigmented oil stain, test the lacquer first. Lacquer will often remove this type of stain if the stain hasn't thoroughly dried.

Begin by flowing the lacquer onto the wood surface in a smooth coat. Spread the lacquer using long strokes without too much back-and-forth brushing. Work rapidly with a wider than normal finishing brush to speed things along. Keep your working area small and finish one area at a time before going on to the next.

After covering the entire surface with lacquer, leave the piece alone for at least 4 hours. The key to success with lacquers is allowing a longer drying time than the label stipulates. Even though your surface will dry dust-free in minutes, 4 hours is the minimum time to wait before sanding or applying a second coat.

Sanding between coats of lacquer is not always necessary for good adhesion. Like shellac, each additional coat of lacquer tends to soften the preceding one, making an excellent chemical bond (unlike the mechanical bond needed when using varnish). However, you may want to sand a lacquer finish anyway with 400-grit sandpaper to level any high spots or to remove other finishing defects.

Repeat lacquer applications as necessary, with at least 4 to 6 hours of drying time between coats. After the final coat of lacquer has dried overnight, you can rub the already glossy surface with pumice or rottenstone and oil for an even higher gloss finish (see Rubbing & Waxing, page 48).

For spray application of lacquer, refer to pages 71-74 for hints on spraying. Be sure to read the manufacturer's directions on both the lacquer and the spray equipment. So many types of sprayers and brands of lacquer are available that it is always wise to experiment before you undertake any important furniture project.

Color and cover with enamel

Decorative painting for protection and durability has been the most widely used form of wood finishing for over 1,000 years. Colored opaque enamel finishes are versatile and easy to apply to any furniture surface. Often opaque finishes are necessary because a clear wood finish would not be practical. You'll probably want to use an opaque finish in the following cases:

• *When the wood you're finishing has a very plain, ordinary grain pattern* that you don't want to accentuate with a stain or a final clear finish.

• *When the furniture you're working on has been constructed from several different kinds of woods.* This combination of woods occurs frequently, especially with old rocking chairs. If new woods are mixed with old, or softwoods are mixed with hardwoods, a final stain and clear finish will only magnify these differences.

• *When the surface of the wood has been extensively damaged.* In many cases, you'll find furniture that has been damaged in a fire but is still serviceable. A colorful coat of enamel will hide these surface defects and give good wood furniture a few more years of use.

• *When you want to match a particular project to its surroundings.* Often a kitchen table is painted a certain color to accent the kitchen decor. Sometimes you might want to add a bright color to an unusually dark spot in your home—interesting colors can brighten any room.

PICK THE PROPER ENAMEL FINISH

A colored enamel finish is usually manufactured in the same way and with the same solvents as a clear finish, but with pigments added. When it comes time for you to decide on a colored finish for a specific project, refer back to the characteristics of the related clear finishes discussed in this chapter; then pick the finish that best suits your needs.

Colored enamel is simply a varnish with pigments added. A good enamel is equal to a good varnish for durability, method of application, and drying time. As with varnish, enamel finishes are available in flat, satin, and glossy surfaces; the glossy is the most durable. Enamels can further be divided into three groups:

• *Alkyd-base enamels* have an oil base and require paint thinner (mineral spirits) as a solvent. These enamels can be used for either indoor or outdoor furniture and they are so durable that they are easy to clean.

• *Polyurethane-base enamels* are extremely tough, resisting abrasion and chipping. Often they, too, are soluble in paint thinner, but it is wise to read the manufacturer's directions for any variations in solvent instructions.

• *Acrylic-base enamels*—also called latex or vinyl enamels—are durable, odorless, nonflammable, and easy to apply. An important advantage is that, with them, you use water as a solvent, making latex easy to thin and to clean up after. These enamels are not available in a high gloss finish, though.

Pigmented shellac, having many of the properties of regular shellac, is often used as a sealer (see Sealing the Surface, page 27). A good application of colored shellac over wood knots and sap streaks prevents them from bleeding through into the final finishing coat. As with regular shel-

Knots frequently hide sap pockets—first clean thoroughly with solvent, then seal with shellac to prevent sap from coming through final finish

lac, colored shellac should be purchased only in the quantity needed for each job, since shellac will deteriorate if stored too long (see The Classic Look of Shellac, page 38).

Colored lacquer, similar to regular lacquer, is available for spraying and brushing. Because lacquer by nature is a thin finish, it is unable to hold very much pigment. For this reason, several coats of lacquer must be applied to properly cover any furniture surface (see Lacquer: Fast, Dust-Free Drying, page 45). Lacquer is especially useful in small aerosol spray cans. The number of colors available in aerosols is almost unlimited, and ease of application makes aerosols especially useful for small projects or parts of a large project where a brush can't conveniently reach.

APPLYING THE COLOR

Whichever finish you choose, apply it to the wood in at least two coats to ensure a good covering job. Many furniture finishers use an undercoat over the bare wood first to better prepare the surface. An undercoat provides a smooth, nonporous initial finish to which the top coat can adhere. If you're in doubt as to the best method to use for the finish you've chosen, be sure to read the manufacturer's directions.

Begin by dipping your brush into the colored finish but don't submerge the bristles more than halfway. Apply the first coat of finish as you would varnish (see Varnish—Durable and Protective, page 43). The first coat is always easier to apply if you lightly thin your product with the solvent the manufacturer recommends. The second coat of finish should always be used directly from the can, unthinned.

Let the first coat dry at least 24 hours (depending on the product), and then sand it lightly with 220-grit open-coat garnet paper before applying the second coat. Allow another 24 hours for the second coat to dry; then apply a third coat if you choose, but only after you have sanded well with 320 to 400-grit sandpaper and wiped the sanding dust away.

The final finish can be rubbed (similar to a varnish or a lacquer—see Rubbing & Waxing, pages 48-49) or it can be left as is. If you want the final surface to be semiglossy, you can use a semigloss finish for the last coat. You'll get a higher quality finish, though, if you use a gloss for all coats and flatten the sheen with sandpaper or steel wool at the end.

...Using enamel

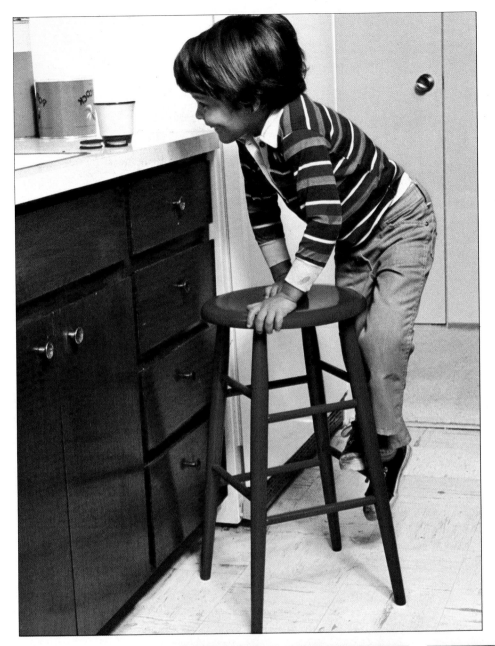

Cookie-scavenging boys *can be hard on kitchen furniture. This red enamel stool can take it, though, and retain its color for years to come.*

Careful sanding *of old finish* **(near right)** *reveals very ordinary white wood used in stool's construction.* **Far right:** *Don't bother to strip old finish off—just sand surface smooth and apply new enamel coat.*

Rubbing & waxing

Rubbing and waxing will add an impressive final touch to any newly finished wood surface.

Careful rubbing with rottenstone, pumice, or fine wet abrasive paper is a way to smooth the surface to produce a perfectly even matte or polished wood finish. For a soft, polished final appearance, use rottenstone (it's only available in one grade). For a duller finish, use FFF-grade pumice (the finest grade) or special wet-sanding abrasive paper (600-grit or finer).

A good paste wax applied after the last abrasive rub and cleanup will further preserve the newly finished surface. Liberally apply a hard, paste-type floor wax to the wood and then buff it by hand or machine for the maximum surface protection and beauty.

Wet sanding *is simple way to smooth surface after final finishing. Soak some abrasive paper in water before wrapping it around sanding block and beginning your wet sanding in the direction of the wood grain.*

1. Pour lubricating oil *directly on surface. Paraffin oil was used here, but any other form of lubrication (even old automotive motor oil) would work just as well.*

2. Sprinkle ground pumice *(FFF-the finest grade is recommended) over newly-oiled surface. Pumice kept in old salt or pepper shaker is easy to apply.*

3. Rub pumice-oil solution *evenly over surface with old blackboard eraser. Apply slight pressure. Use same application method with rotten-stone for glossier surface shine.*

4. Spoon paste wax *onto moist rag or sock to make fine applicator for wax coating. Dark-colored waxes are available for special use on dark-colored pieces of furniture.*

5. Rub wax evenly *over wood surface. Use slight pressure with your hand to push paste wax deep down into any open wood pores. Wipe surface clean.*

6. Polish newly-waxed surface *with soft cloth or power electric buffer having felt or lambswool pad. Pressing lightly will prevent buffing all the wax away.*

Child's room *glows with hint of nostalgia as antique blue rocking chair waits patiently for little boy to fetch his bear.*

1. Sanding furniture *is not crucial, but the surface must be smooth for the finish to adhere.*

2. Paint piece *with base coat using good opaque enamel. Be sure to cover all surfaces.*

3. Apply glaze toner *to dry paint with a brush, then wipe toner off with clean rag.*

Special decorating methods

An array of unusual finishing techniques

Novelty wood finishes are the answer when you want to add sparkle to an otherwise ordinary furniture piece. Easy to do and distinctive, novelty finishes can open up a whole new world of decorating techniques.

Remember, though, that *decorating* furniture is not always the same as *finishing* furniture. Decoration itself often provides no protection for the wood surface. However, one or two coats of a clear final finish over the decoration will often give the wood all the protection it needs.

An imaginative wood finisher can come up with many creative ideas for novelty effects; you probably come in contact with a few of them every day without even realizing it.

The strip around the edge of a table, the animal decals on your child's dresser, or the new "antique" chair that you just purchased from a local furniture store—all pieces have some added surface decoration that sets their finish apart from a more standard wood covering.

The simple art of antiquing

Also known as "highlighting," "shading," and "glazing," antiquing is a simple way to simulate an old or time-worn appearance. This technique is especially effective when used on inexpensive, unfinished furniture or over any poor quality furniture woods.

To "antique" any piece of furniture is really no more complicated than applying a thin coat of one color paint over a base coat of another color; the thin coat (glaze) is then lightly wiped away as it dries, revealing a slightly two-tone effect with the base coat color showing through.

Never use antiquing on high quality furniture or even over slightly damaged or well-worn antiques. Whenever you have an interesting wood grain with a wood surface in reasonably good shape, always choose a clear finish to emphasize the furniture's beauty and originality.

When the quality of the furniture is in question, though, or when the surface has been badly damaged or already has an old finish that you'd rather not remove, a good antique finish will give the furniture a new lease on life.

YOUR OPTIONS IN FINISHES

Many paint and hardware stores sell ready-made antiquing kits in color-coordinated shades. Produced by paint manufacturers, these kits often provide everything you need for a successful final finish.

Included in each kit you'll usually find a base color, a color-matched top glaze, and complete instructions. A kit may also contain sandpaper, brushes, and other miscellaneous small items.

The base coats supplied in these kits range from colorful opaque enamels to subtle wood-tone shades. Glazes, often selected to contrast with the base

Distressing gives a well-aged look

When furniture is "distressed," it is artificially aged or worn. Distressing is a popular masquerade for new, unfinished furniture, as well as for wood that shows few signs of ever having been used.

Many imitators of antiques use knives, rasps, and abrasives to simulate wear; rough grinding wheels and key chains to produce nicks and gouges; and small drills or nails to give the effect of wood-boring worms. With these new "old" markings, a recently built piece of furniture can be turned into something that looks old and valuable.

Since the technique of distressing is not a finishing technique, all surfaces should be distressed before a final finishing coat is applied. Distressing is more useful when combined with other decorating effects, such as antiquing or scorching (see page 54).

You can simulate wear and tear on furniture by using practically any hard object—a rock, an old nail, a heavy tool, or a chain. Here are a few suggestions for giving furniture a pleasingly distressed appearance:

• Worn edges, probably the most obvious signs of age in furniture, can be simulated with the use of files, rasps, and sandpaper. Any worn spot you add should be placed in a natural "high-use" area of the furniture—a corner rounded from years of moving, a chair rung flattened by many shoes, and so on.

• Worm holes can be simulated with small nails, drill bits, ice picks, or even a shotgun blast of birdshot at 30 feet. Such holes are most often found around the legs of tables and chairs—the first spot where hungry worms might be found.

• Dents in the surface can be made by heavy stones, keys, chains, or a small hammer. Make sure you use a blunt object, though—you don't want to tear the wood fibers.

With a little imagination, the resourceful furniture finisher can create many other distressed effects. When all surface dents and abrasions have been made, lightly sand any rough edges to give the marks a slightly more natural appearance.

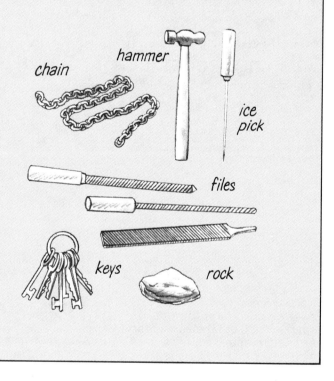

chain hammer ice pick files keys rock

---

coat, are available in white, gold, brown, black, and other colors.

Some paint stores sell base coats and glazes separately. If you're interested in making up your own antiquing kit, use any good semigloss enamel as the base and choose a coordinated color glaze. Some of the most popular color choices for antique finishes are a bright red base coat glazed with black, a blue base glazed with white, and an olive green base glazed with brown.

PREPARING THE SURFACE

A major advantage of applying an antique finish to previously finished furniture is that it often eliminates the need for removing the old finish. As long as the old finish on your furniture is in good condi-

tion and isn't cracking or peeling, simply clean it well with detergent and water to remove dirt and wipe it with denatured alcohol to eliminate excessive wax buildup.

Consider most blemishes or dents you find in the old finish to be assets. If the damages are below the wood surface, they'll catch a larger share of the glaze coat and stand out clearly for that highlighted, well-worn look.

In some old finishes, though, there will be ugly scratches that you'd rather not highlight with the new finish. Remove these marks by entirely removing the old finish or at least spot-sanding the area until the particular blemish disappears.

When antiquing unfinished furniture, you may want to make a few deliberate surface blemishes

first just to give the piece a used look. Whenever there is a definite lack of character in your wood surface, you can always add visual interest with a little loving abuse inflicted by any number of common household objects (see Distressing Gives a Well-Aged Look, above).

APPLYING THE BASE COAT

If your furniture has previously been given an opaque color and the finish is still in good condition, you already have an excellent antiquing base. It won't matter either if the original paint job was less than perfect because quite often a few erratic brush marks will add to the top glaze's one-of-a-kind look.

If a new semigloss base is

needed, sand the wood thoroughly and apply the base just as you would any regular enamel (see Color & Cover with Enamel, page 46). Furniture woods that absorb most of the first semigloss coat may require a second coat. Carefully sand between base coats—all glazes naturally adhere better to the dull shine of a good semigloss base.

Spraying on your base coat with good spray equipment is even easier than brushing it on (see Spray Gun Finishing, page 72). If you do a lot of antiquing, a spray gun is a sound investment. But if the antique colors you're looking for are also available in aerosol spray cans, a can will be far more convenient than a spray gun for small, delicate projects.

APPLYING THE GLAZE

Once the base coat has dried, brush the antique glaze liberally over every square inch of furniture surface. Gradually work the glaze into all cracks, corners, molding details, and blemishes or "character" marks in the base coat. When the wood surface has been thoroughly soaked, let the glaze dry until it begins to dull; then start gently wiping away the excess glaze with a soft cloth.

WIPING THE GLAZE

Begin wiping in the center of each flat surface and work towards the outside edges, wiping with the grain. Be sure to wipe the glaze away from high spots on the surface but leave some in surface indentations. Wiping the glaze in this manner highlights those areas where furniture would naturally show wear. Also try to leave some of the glaze in corners, on edges, and in molding details to accent and add dimension to the final finish.

After the glaze has been lightly wiped to your satisfaction, there are a number of other novelty techniques that will let you obtain an even more unusual finish. Three of these, described in the following paragraphs, are graining, stippling, and crosshatching. Always practice these techniques on a piece of scrap wood first before trying them on your particular project:

Graining results from dragging the tips of a dry, stiff-bristle brush or a piece of fine (4/0) steel wool across the partially wiped glaze surface. This creates a slightly wood-textured appearance that can often make a painted surface actually look like an old, weathered piece of wood.

Stippling the freshly glazed surface often produces a random wood grain pattern. To stipple, lightly touch the surface with either a dry sponge or a wadded paper towel. Applying crumpled newsprint to the wet glaze often results in a pebbly, marbleized surface.

Crosshatching consists of laying canvas cloth or burlap onto the newly glazed surface and then removing it. The harder you press down on the burlap, the more pronounced the decorative, weave-like effect will be. Use your imagination to think up other novelty wiping techniques.

SEALING THE FINISH

When the glaze coat is completely dry (usually in 48 to 72 hours), it is always a good idea to seal the surface with a clear, protective finish. This sealing prevents the glaze from chipping off and gives better overall protection to any additional surface decorations you may have applied (see Stenciling and Striping, page 57).

To achieve the best clear finish over a glaze, choose a good semigloss varnish—or even a glossy varnish, if you want a high shine (see Varnish—Durable and Protective, page 43).

To add interesting antiqued effects...

Simulate wood grain by drawing the tip of a dry brush across the wet glaze

Pad mottled patterns onto the newly glazed surface with a dry sponge or paper towel

Make cross-hatch patterns by pressing burlap or canvas onto the wet glaze surface

Scorching: fire can add new life

A scorched finish—often called "charring" or "burning" the surface—is the result of lightly applying the flame from a propane torch to a bare wood surface. Propane gas torches are versatile tools, excellent for small crafts and repairs around the home. After scorching, the wood appears to be stained an attractive deep brown or black color, though the colors differ according to the varying hardness of the wood grain.

Scorching is never used on choice hardwoods or on furniture of any great value. As you might guess, this technique virtually destroys the wood surface, making it nearly impossible to restore the wood to its original condition.

You might find scorching useful, though, on pieces of unfinished furniture or on anything else made from such softer woods as fir and pine—rough 2" by 4" softwood furniture, for example.

Before you apply the propane torch flame to the furniture surface, make sure all wood is clean and dry, bare of any inflammable solvents or old finish, and in generally good repair. Be sure to remove all knobs, drawer pulls, mirrors, and anything else that might be damaged by the heat.

Apply the propane flame to the wood with a smooth, back and forth motion of your hand. Keep the torch moving at an even distance from the surface and direct the controlled blue flame exactly where you want it. Avoid using the center core, which is the hottest part of the torch flame, or the

flame may burn the wood surface too deeply.

The purpose of this first step is to produce an even, overall charring of the wood, penetrating only

To start a propane torch...

1. Screw torch burner to propane cylinder fitting

2. Open control valve just enough to let a small amount of gas escape

3. Immediately light the torch and allow the burner to become fully heated before opening valve for a larger flame

deeply enough to scorch the outside wood grain. If small circles of yellow flame flare up from the surface, you're burning too deeply. Quickly pull the torch away and try to avoid this area during further flaming.

When scorching sharp edges, be careful not to let them remain too long under the intense heat of the flame. Inside corners also demand special care because the propane flame is often not pointed enough to reach into the deepest nooks and crannies of your furniture.

Brush the wood briskly in the direction of the wood grain when charring is completed. Use a stiff-bristle wire brush, available at all paint and hardware stores, to remove the soft char from between the hard wood and soft wood on the newly scorched surface.

Continue your scorching and brushing until the surface is free of all loose charcoal and the wood texture has a uniform color. To obtain a final sheen, go over the surface with fine steel wool or extra-fine abrasive paper to emphasize the hardgrain ridges and the softwood valleys in the wood's surface.

Finish the scorched surface by applying two or three coats of a hard paste wax and polishing thoroughly (see Rubbing & Waxing, pages 48-49). If the newly burned surface is a table or anything else that will be in constant use, apply a thick coat of clear polyurethane varnish instead of wax for added surface protection (see Varnish—Durable and Protective, page 43).

Gilding for the Midas touch

Gilding, or applying gold to wood, has been a decorative art since the beginnings of civilization. Ancient artifacts recovered from Egyptian tombs reveal extensive gilding of royal and religious wooden jewelry and symbols. In many cases, gilding techniques that were popular in ancient Egypt are still used today.

Gold leafing is perhaps the most traditional method for applying gold to wood. Because 22-carat gold leaf is often less than one quarter of one thousandth of an inch thick, though, it is usually quite difficult to apply. Its high cost also places gold leaf out of the financial range of many a beginning do-it-yourself finisher.

Powder gilding or "bronzing" has largely taken the place of leaf gilding because it is less expensive and easier to apply. But powder gilding is not nearly as durable as gold leaf because it has a less metallic appearance and dulls more quickly than leaf gilding.

Wax gilding is a recent technique

(Continued on page 59)

...Scorching

Scorched pine mirror frame *is a distinctive, practical wall hanging for any room.*

1. Begin by applying flame *carefully from propane torch to wood surface.*

2. Next, use stiff wire brush *to remove all soft charred wood from between hardgrain ridges.*

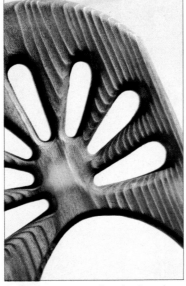

3. Close-up reveals *wire brush marks on soft surface. Raised hardgrain is barely burned.*

4. Finish wood *with protective clear coating, emphasizing dimension and beauty of textured wood grain.*

Stenciling & striping

Stenciling is as easy as cutting a design from a stiff piece of paper and then using short bursts of spray paint to leave the intended pattern anywhere you choose. Create children's names, floral patterns, or modern pop art motifs as the whim suits you. Restore the original stenciling designs to the back of an old Hitchcock chair or a special Pennsylvania Dutch piece.

Striping is also extremely simple. If you look around at many pieces of furniture, you'll find a basic decorative stripe to be far more widely used than you had at first imagined. Although intricate spider web striping designs are difficult without a certain amount of practice, simple edge lining—the major striping used on furniture today—is fairly easy to do.

Stenciling and striping allow you to use color with a contemporary flair to decorate many plain wooden pieces. Personalize them, identify them, give them character, or just make them fun to have around—the choice is up to you.

Rainbow stool *could be a boy's pride and joy. Decorate it any way you like—with a clear protective covering, such as a thick polyurethane varnish, it should show few if any signs of wear.*

1. Draw and cut stencil out of heavy paper—small manicure scissors or sharp razor craft knife and cutting board are recommended.

2. Spray chosen stencil color onto newspaper and stencil-covered stool. Don't hold spray can too close; be sure to keep it moving so you won't build up heavy drips in one spot. Peel papers away when paint is not quite dry.

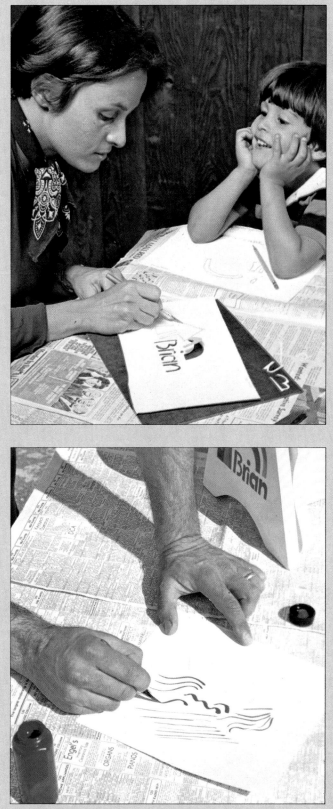

3. Stripe practice scrap of paper before you begin. If you use special striping brush (available at craft stores), you can draw variety of lines by changing turn of your wrist and angle of brush to surface.

4. Steady your striping brush on project with your third and little finger. Simple edge lining is probably easiest decoration to do. You may wish to try other, more complicated decorations as you become more experienced.

...Gilding

Gold picture frame *stylishly accents classic portrait of French lady being fitted in place over fireplace.*

1. To restore old frame, *begin by dusting it thoroughly with soft, clean paint brush.*

2. Repair any chips *or breaks in gesso design with a mixture of plaster of Paris, water, and white glue.*

3. Apply gold leaf paint *to repairs with small artist's brush. Doing this will provide good base for wax gilt.*

4. Freshen entire frame *with wax gilt by dipping soft cloth into turpentine and then into small amount of gilt.*

...Continued from page 54

that is now considered to be the most popular gilding method. Sold in cosmetic-type jars, this gold paste may be easily rubbed onto the wood surface with one's fingers or a cloth and then buffed to a beautiful sheen with another soft cloth. Such excellent results are produced by this inexpensive product, which so closely resembles fine gold leaf, that wax gold is virtually the only gilding method worth using by the occasional wood finisher.

PROJECT SUGGESTIONS

Almost any wooden object can be enhanced by gilding. Try these subtle gold effects on the elegant carvings of an old chair or on a new jewelry box you've made for yourself. Once you understand the basic fundamentals of gilding, you'll be amazed at the many possible uses you'll find for this attractive technique.

Today, most gilding is applied to wooden picture frames that have plaster designs. If you discover an old frame around the house that needs minor repairs or regilding, choose this for the perfect project to practice on.

PREPARING THE SURFACE

All picture frames must be thoroughly cleaned before you begin to gild. Start cleaning by brushing the entire frame with a soft, clean paintbrush to remove any dust in the frame's design. Spots which are unusually dirty may be rubbed with a cloth that has been lightly moistened in water and then wrung as dry as possible. Always clean a frame carefully because any excessive dampness may loosen the water-soluble glues holding the plaster design to the wood.

REPAIRING THE DESIGN

If your picture frame has any broken or missing parts, you'll have to repair or replace them first. The majority of all ornate details on "carved" wooden frames are really not carved from wood at all. Instead, during construction a plasterlike material is formed into designs and bonded to the frame's wooden base. This material is called "gesso"—a hard

substance similar to plaster that you can easily make yourself. The process is much simpler than you might think (see following instructions); you can easily mix new gesso to make either small constructions for minor repairs or molds if several details are missing.

Gesso dries quickly and provides an excellent surface to which gilt can adhere. And gesso is versatile: it will accept almost any finish, such as shellac, lacquer, paint, varnish, or wax. (All of these finishes can be removed with appropriate solvents without harming the gesso design itself.) A disadvantage of gesso is its vulnerability to chips, dents, and hairline cracks as the material ages and becomes worn.

Mix gesso from plaster of Paris, water, and a little water-soluble white glue. Work quickly because gesso will begin to set within about 3 minutes after you've started. Discard the mix as soon as you notice a crumbly quality developing—only smooth gesso will hold securely.

Use the smallest glass dish you can find to mix gesso—a liquor shot glass is perfect—and only make a small amount at a time. Since gesso will dry far too quickly to be used if made in large quantities, you may have to make over 50 individual small batches of the mixture to repair a large frame with many defects.

Begin by pouring 1/2 teaspoon of plaster of Paris into your glass dish. Add a little water with an eyedropper and a little water-soluble white glue; then stir the mixture thoroughly with a small, flat piece of wood. Too much water in the mixture will make the gesso runny so that it can't be worked with the fingers. Too much glue will give the gesso a shiny look and make it brittle and difficult to sand or carve after it dries.

When it comes to making the right gesso mixture, experience will be your best teacher.

Make a construction by applying a thin layer of undiluted white glue to the spot on the frame you wish to repair. Next, mix the gesso as explained above. Remove the gesso from the glass dish, roll it into a little puttylike ball between your fingers, and quickly apply it to the damaged area on the frame. Shape the gesso with your

finger to match the shape of the surrounding design. Pottery tools, icepicks, and toothpicks are especially helpful in forming elaborate designs with gesso.

When the fresh gesso area has dried overnight, sand it gently to size with 220-grit abrasive paper. Then paint on a light coat of pure orange shellac in order to seal the repair from moisture.

Making a "mold" is similar to making a construction except that a mold is used only when a large part of the frame design is missing. If one decorated corner of a picture frame is gone but at least one other corner is still intact, make a mold of the existing original corner to form a replacement gesso design for the corner that's damaged.

To make a gesso mold...

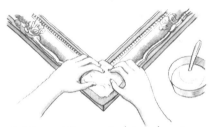

1. *Mix molding material and apply to unbroken design*

2. *When set, carefully peel mold off design and fill with newly mixed gesso*

3. *When new piece is dry, separate from mold, shape to fit, and glue to void in frame*

Good molding materials take clear impressions of the finest details and often remain flexible long after use. Probably the best molding product is the gel-like substance used by dentists for making teeth impressions. Available at many craft stores or dental supply firms, this excellent product mixes with water, sets quickly, and is easy to apply to the surface you wish to copy. Always be sure to follow the manufacturer's directions for mixing and use.

After you have placed a mold on the design, peel the molding material off the frame as soon as it will easily release (usually in 3 to 15 minutes). Mix a fairly large batch of gesso until it has the consistency of whipped cream; pour it into the mold. When the gesso has hardened (usually after several hours) discard the original molding material. Allow the new gesso mold to dry overnight before you attempt any further work on it.

All gesso molds should come out of the molding material with a smooth top surface that needs no sanding. The bottom of the gesso mold should always be sanded, though, so that the gesso will rest evenly on the frame.

If necessary, use light carving to blend the mold's design into the existing frame design. A sharp razor craft knife will help take off any extra gesso, but remember to use slow, short strokes to prevent breaking the mold.

Fix scrapes and abrasions on your plaster design with any extra gesso left over from your repairs. As you continue to work on various constructions and molds, any gesso remaining on your hands should be smoothed over small surface marks with your fingers. If a blemish is large, apply the gesso over a thin glue base. Since runny gesso is perfect for filling cracks and little holes, you may be able to use a poorly made mixture in this way.

APPLYING THE GILT

Whether your plans call for regilding a newly repaired picture frame or decorating from scratch an unfinished wooden novelty item, the process of wax gilding is just about the same. All gilding has a better appearance when it is applied over a smooth gesso base.

Prepare a good base for the gilt by lightly sanding the gesso repairs and applying a thin coat of orange shellac. Shellac serves to waterproof the water-soluble glue under the gesso and prevents the gesso from coming loose from the wood base.

Paint over the gesso next with a high-quality liquid gold leaf paint. Don't purchase a so-called "gilt" paint because these are usually poorly made and runny, and contain no real gold. If you always insist on the liquid gold leaf available at most artists' supply and craft stores, your gilding will have the brilliance and durability of "real" gold. You'll find liquid gold leaf to be relatively inexpensive.

Gold leaf paint is most useful when you apply it to a small area to match a newly repaired surface to the original finish. If gold leaf paint is applied to large, flat surfaces, a pattern of irregular brush marks will detract from the overall effect.

Apply gold leaf paint with a 1/2" flat bristle or camel's hair art brush. Work quickly because most liquid leaf paints contain a base similar to that of shellac, which causes them to dry sooner than you might expect.

Freshen the entire project with wax gilt when the liquid leaf has dried. Wax gilt is available in cosmetic-size jars at the same artists' supply and craft stores at which liquid gold leaf is sold. It is relatively inexpensive.

True wax gilt is often made from real gold suspended in a turpentine and wax base. Wax gilt can also come in many colors, including white gold, rose gold, silver gold, and brass. Be sure to choose the color that most closely resembles the surrounding areas you are trying to match.

If you are working on an old gilt picture frame, you'll probably want to freshen the entire project. When a project is newer, though, you usually won't be gilding the whole thing so use wax gilt only on the highlights.

You apply wax gilt by dipping a small piece of soft cloth in a little turpentine and then in the jar of wax gilt. Apply the gilt over the liquid leaf base, as well as over any remaining original gold leaf. Use the pressure of your finger during application to bring out the depth of the wax gilt's color. For large areas use a small nylon flat-bristle brush, dipped first in a small amount of turpentine and then in the wax. Brush back and forth over the surface until you obtain the desired sheen.

When your entire project has been covered with wax gilt, use a soft cloth to buff the "real" gold to a truly resplendent appearance. Don't use too much wax, though—a little goes a long way.

ANTIQUING GILT FINISHES FOR INTEREST

On many picture frames and other novelty gilding projects, the "new" gold look needs to be subdued or aged. Antiquing a gilt frame is similar to antiquing any regular furniture finish (see The Simple Art of Antiquing, page 51).

Choose the right toner by asking your paint dealer specifically for a furniture antiquing toner with a brownish tint. Frequently the toner you buy will be a thick, creamy mixture just as it comes from the paint dealer's toning machine. Take it home and mix it as needed, with 3 parts of its recommended solvent to 1 part toner.

Apply the toner liberally around the entire gilt surface. Brush it deep into all designs, depressions, and surface irregularities. Then quickly wipe the majority of the toner away with a soft, dry cloth to reveal the gilt highlights. Use a dry brush to get down into the surface details and depressions in order to create a "grainy" effect in darker areas.

Highlight the raised spots in the design by adding a little more wax gilt after the toner has dried. Rub the gilt in right from the jar with your fingers. You can go over the entire project again if you like, but don't put more gilt down into the detailed areas—you'll want your toner left there to form shadows.

When finished, buff the surface with a clean, soft cloth to bring out the natural brilliance and deep shine of antiqued gold.

Creative? Try découpage

Découpage is the technique of mounting pictures or designs on wooden or metal surfaces and then covering them with a clear finish.

Either bare wood or previously finished wood can be used as a base for découpage because, after several clear finishing coats are applied, the pictures or designs will appear to be part of the surface itself.

Almost any object that is flat enough to be glued down can be used for découpage. Photographs, pieces of fabric, yarns, illustrations, wedding invitations, stamps, and postcards are perfectly suitable for découpage, and will add appeal to decorative plaques, children's furniture, and many other wooden surfaces.

Choose any background color that pleases you for your découpage. Solid colors, stains, or natural wood tones work well. The main consideration is to complement whatever design you have chosen.

PREPARING THE DESIGN

Though there is no one "best" way of preparing an object for découpage, there are several techniques used by those who enjoy this craft:

Outlining is one of the easiest methods for preparing a print to be used in découpage. All you have to do is to cut around the entire main subject of the print with scissors or a razor-sharp craft knife to eliminate the background. On the other hand, you may want to leave some of the background intact; it often adds proportion and interest to the central subject.

If you select a picture to be outlined, try choosing one that is not too highly detailed. A simple, neatly cut picture will give you much more enjoyment than a detailed one that ends up poorly cut. If your design does have a lot of detail, though, try tearing it roughly away from the background. The torn, ragged edges can often mute the scissor sharpness of many intricate lines.

Burning the edges of a design with a cigarette, candle, match, or lighter is also an interesting way of framing a découpage picture. Hold the design face up and level (or loosely roll it up) as you pass the edges over a flame. As soon as the paper catches fire, blow out the flame. Continue in the same way around all edges of the print until the desired charred effect is completed.

For charring edges of a design...

roll design into a loose cylinder and carefully apply burning match to each end

Thinning your découpage item is necessary if you plan to use a very heavy piece of paper, such as a menu or a postcard. Stripping away some of the thickness of the design will allow you to cover it more easily with a final clear finish.

To protect the design before thinning, first apply a thin, clear film over the face of it. (Check with local craft stores to determine which product to use.) Then place the design in a pan of warm water and let it soak. As the water cools, gently roll the various layers of paper off the back of the design one thickness at a time; then press the design flat between two pieces of absorbent paper and allow enough time for the design to dry.

Printing on the back of a design will often show through after the design has been glued to a wooden surface. Whenever possible, avoid designs with printing on the back. If you have no choice, seal the back of the design *first* with a heavy coat of white glue diluted slightly with water.

PREPARING THE SURFACE

Now that your design is ready, the next step in découpaging is to make sure that the wood surface you plan to decorate is completely smooth and clean. Fill all blemishes with wood dough or putty (see Scars and Nicks, page 19) and sand the surface smooth with 180-grit or finer aluminum oxide abrasive paper.

Découpage can be mounted just as easily on stained wood or on a clear or colored protective finish as it can be on bare wood. Choose a base color that complements the design you've selected and apply it according to the instructions given on pages 31 or 46. When using an opaque finish, you may need to apply at least two or more separate coats to adequately cover the wood grain. Sand lightly if necessary between finish coats.

Always choose the final clear finish you will be applying over your design at the same time you select a base. Good possible combinations include enamels and enamel undercoat bases under polyurethane varnishes, and artist's acrylics or pigmented vinyl stain bases under a spray can lacquer finish.

If you are découpaging over antiquing (see The Simple Art of Antiquing, page 51), the design may be applied either *under* the glaze or *over* the glaze before the final clear finish.

When découpaging over bare wood, apply a thin coat of top finish first before placing the design; then lightly sand with 220-grit abrasive paper to remove any surface irregularities.

APPLYING THE DESIGN

When you've chosen and prepared your design, place it on the smoothed wood surface and, with a pencil, lightly mark the intended location of the design. Lift the design off the surface and lay it face down on a clean piece of common kitchen plastic wrap. (If you use wax paper over the design instead of common plastic wrap, some of the wax may stick to the design's surface and prevent the final finish from adhering.) Apply white glue (or a small amount of tacky, moist material, such as the final finish you've chosen) to the back of the design, spreading it around evenly with your fingers. (On a larger surface, use a damp sponge to spread the glue.)

The design should then be carefully lifted from the plastic wrap and placed on the wood surface according to the previous pencil marks. Lightly press the design in place.

When the design is properly aligned, place a clean piece of kitchen plastic wrap over the design and use a hard rubber roller (available in photography stores) to press out all excess glue.

Remove the top layer of plastic wrap and clean around the edges of the design with a damp sponge. Place a clean piece of plastic wrap over the design, roll again, and wipe off additional excess glue. Repeat this process until no more glue appears around the design's edges.

Any glue you leave on the surface will result in cloudy spots on the wood, especially if your project has a dark base. A good, clear finish will usually obscure these clouds. But if they're bad enough to bother you, carefully rub the wood around the edges of the découpage design with 4/0 steel wool.

Allow your project to dry overnight. If air bubbles appear in the design by morning, slit each with a razor blade and apply glue under the cut edges with a toothpick. Roll the design once more under clean plastic wrap and let everything dry again.

Before applying the final finish, you can personalize your newly découpaged wood, if you like. Add a few words, the date, or possibly even sign your name to your design, using black India ink or paint for best results. Make sure

all writing is completely dry before proceeding with the finishing coat. Save all additional decorations that are too thick to be covered by a finish until later, after the finish has been applied.

APPLYING THE FINISH

Once the design has been glued to the wood surface and has dried, you're ready to apply the final finish.

You've probably planned ahead what your final coat will be (see page 7), but if you happen to have used a noncomplementary base coat, change the final finishing coat *now* to avoid problems in the future.

Begin applying your chosen finish. For specific application techniques, refer to those other areas in this book where clear finishes are discussed in detail:
- Catalytic sealer—page 37
- Shellac—page 38
- Polyurethane varnish—page 43
- Lacquer—page 45
- Antiquing glaze—page 51

Continue applying finishing coats until you have built up an adequate protective surface over the design. After enough of the finish has been applied, lightly wet sand the surface with 400—600 grit sandpaper to remove all of the surface shine.

Wipe off the sanding residue and apply more finishing coats, if you desire. Between subsequent coats, do a little more light sanding, constantly wiping the dry surface with a soft cloth to remove any dust.

The number of finish coats you'll need for a smooth surface is often a matter of personal opinion. Depending on the thickness of your design and the rate of absorption of the finish into the wood, you should apply a minimum of 6 coats of finish. Polyurethane, a thick finish, may often take fewer coats, but if you use an extremely thin finish, such as spray lacquer, a minimum of 12 coats is usually recommended.

If your final finish is glossy and you'd like a satin sheen instead, rub the surface with 3/0 or 4/0 or finer steel wool once the finish has dried. When the finish appears uniformly dull, protect the surface with one or two coats of a good paste wax, polishing with a clean, soft cloth.

...Découpage

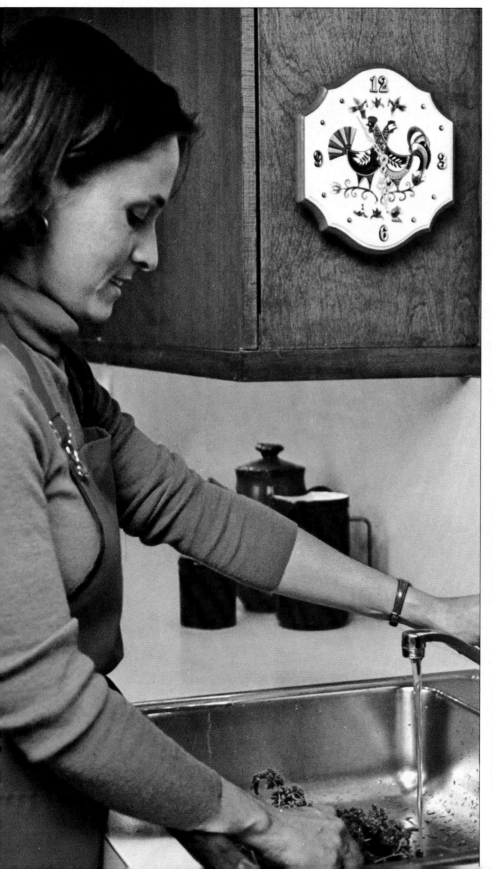

Découpaged wall clock *is fun addition to any room. Look for battery-operated movement in clock shop or mail-order catalog.*

1. Cut your chosen design *away from its background with small scissors or razor-sharp craft knife.*

2. Apply design *to new surface with ordinary white glue. Use plastic kitchen wrap and roller to flatten.*

3. Brush on clear finish, *being careful to lightly cover sides as well as face of design.*

4. Wet sand surface smooth *with 400-grit abrasive after applying a number of protective coats.*

Padding a blemish *is much easier than refinishing entire project. Even if it doesn't work, you've lost nothing by trying.*

Alligatoring *is frequently caused by expansion and contraction of old finish. Reamalgamation is one way to repair this condition.*

Dark spots *are severe water or ink marks that have penetrated through finish and have dried in wood pores.*

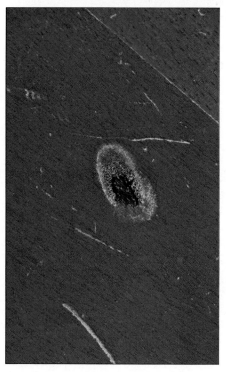

Burn marks *are most frequently caused by cigarettes.*

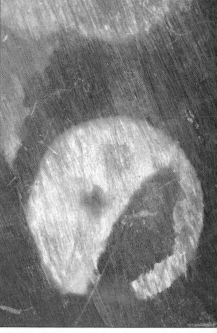

White spots *are caused by moisture in finish.*

New life for an old finish

Patching up: it's easier than refinishing

Old furniture that appears to need refinishing can often be restored with a minimum of effort if you simply repair the original finish. Remember, though, that the charm of old furniture often comes from the same signs of age and use that make a finish look worn out. Be careful of those marks!

Even though a total refinishing job can make your wood look like new, it may have the undesired effect of destroying the character of the piece. By patching up the original finish instead of refinishing, you can usually preserve the authentic quality of the furniture and, at the same time, save yourself a great deal of effort and energy.

The finishing remedies suggested in this chapter apply only to clear finishes—the type that most people have on furniture in their homes. Wooden walls, floors, kitchen cabinets, and so-called "junk" furniture, which is covered with coat after coat of paint, cannot be quite so easily repaired. For suggestions on how to recoat painted furniture, see Color & Cover with Enamel, page 46.

Preparing the surface

Before you begin a full-scale refinishing of any piece of blemished furniture, clean the old surface thoroughly and try to repair the existing finish. If repairs to the old finish don't produce the "new finish" effect you had in mind, then you'll have to take the time to strip, sand, stain, and reapply a final clear protective coat. Either way, you've nothing to lose and you'll learn a great deal about proper finish maintenance in the process.

Determine what finish is on the wood by using the following tests before beginning any repair.
• *Test for shellac:* Apply a little denatured alcohol to some out-of-the-way spot on the surface of your furniture to see if the old finish dissolves; if it does, it's shellac. If your furniture was built before 1920 and still has the original finish, you can be fairly certain it has been finished with shellac.
• *Test for lacquer:* Apply lacquer thinner to a scuffed or worn spot on the surface to see if the finish

dissolves; if it does, it's lacquer. Furniture built after 1920, unless custom-made or previously refinished, usually has a lacquer finish.
• *Test for varnish:* Once a varnish finish has dried, it will not redissolve. Try softening the finish with lacquer thinner or commercial paint remover. If it cracks and raises from the surface, you'll know it's varnish.

Varnish has never been widely used as a finish on commercially built furniture because it dries so slowly. However, you may find a varnish finish on custom-made, handmade, or previously refinished pieces.

Clean the wood surface of the furniture next with a rag lightly moistened with paint thinner (mineral spirits) or turpentine. Or, try a very mild solution of ammonia and water, if you choose. Since ammonia often dissolves shellac though, be sure you've tested the finish on your furniture before cleaning it.

Alternatives to refinishing

Regardless of the type of finishing defect on your furniture, most damage can be easily repaired. The finish repair methods described here are listed in order of increasing difficulty. Be sure to practice any method first in an inconspicuous place before beginning work on more visible areas.

If you use one of the five most popular methods—abrasion, overcoating, reamalgamation, padding, or patching—your wood surface could be beautifully protected in less time than it takes to read this chapter.

ABRASION

Furniture finishes are usually much thicker than most people realize. A shellac, lacquer, or varnish finish is often 1/50 to 1/30 of an inch thick and very tough. Sometimes a finish is so tough that blemishes, such as white spots or water rings, only penetrate through the top 5 percent of the surface coat.

The technique of abrasion wears away this damaged top 5 percent to reveal the undamaged 95 percent of the finish underneath. To scrape the surface, use steel wool (3/0 or 4/0 grade is best) and a little paraffin, oil, motor oil, or linseed oil as lubrication. With these materials, you will be able to remove stains and give wood a new, clear surface without a complete refinishing.

Never use an abrasive paper for abrasion, regardless of how finely textured the paper's grit. Abrasive paper can easily cut through any finish and into the bare wood long before you realize the damage you've done.

Prepare the surface of your piece for light abrasion by cleaning off any wax or oil-base polish that may have built up over the years. Use paint thinner, applying it liberally to the wood with a soft, clean rag.

Next, take part of a pad of 4/0 steel wool, dip it lightly in the lubricant of your choice, and rub back and forth on the surface in the direction of the wood grain. Adjust the pressure of rubbing to the needs of the job at hand. Continue rubbing over and over white spots and other minor surface imperfections until they have been worn away. As soon as a blemish disappears, stop rubbing—you don't want to rub through the finish to the bare wood. When all defects have been removed and the finish looks like new, wipe off the surface with a dry rag and wax with a quality paste wax.

OVERCOATING

In many cases a finish may be completely worn-out—or at least worn in certain spots—and too thin to protect the wood surface anymore. Overcoating is the simple technique of applying a new finish over the remaining serviceable base of the old finish.

When a finish gets old and thin, often not enough is left to repair by the abrasion technique. There may also be a few spots on the surface that are worn not only through the finish but also through the wood stain under the finish. These areas must be touched up before any new finishing overcoat can be applied.

Begin by cleaning the entire surface with paint thinner or with a weak solution of ammonia and water to remove any previous surface wax or polish. If the original stain has worn through in any areas, retouch these spots first by applying just enough new stain to match the surrounding wood.

When the stained areas have thoroughly dried, apply the new finishing coat. Choose any clear finish for the overcoat—shellac, varnish, or lacquer, for example—but try not to apply a modern synthetic varnish over shellac; the results often will not be satisfactory.

Varnishes, however, are the most popular finishes for overcoating because they are easy to apply and exceptionally durable. If you're in doubt about whether or not to apply a certain finish, always test a small amount on some hidden portion of the furniture first to check the effect.

When you've completed the overcoating and it has had a chance to dry, wipe the surface with the finest steel wool you can find; then apply a coat of paste wax for extra protection.

REAMALGAMATION

Whenever your furniture still has a good finish that is only slightly damaged in some way, use the technique of reamalgamation to restore the wood's original beauty. This procedure consists of dissolving and reapplying the finish with some of the finish's original solvent. Reamalgamation is an easy process, and its results are often remarkably successful.

First, use the tests previously described on page 65 to determine exactly what kind of finish is on your furniture. Then clean the surface thoroughly with paint thinner to remove any old polish or wax that has built up.

Begin reamalgamating the old finish by dipping a piece of fine steel wool or a flat-bristle brush into the appropriate solvent and applying it to the wood surface. Try to get as much of the surface wet as quickly as possible before the solvent has a chance to evaporate.

Continue brushing or rubbing in the solvent until all the surface defects disappear. Then apply more solvent to the surface and try to smooth the newly reamalgamated finish with long, light strokes in the direction of the wood grain.

You'll find the solvent will dry almost instantly, leaving a finish that looks like new. When the surface has thoroughly dried, rub it with fresh pieces of 4/0 steel wool to remove any remaining rough spots. Apply a good paste wax as final protection.

PADDING

Padding is the refinishing term that describes the technique of applying a new finish over an old one using a tightly rolled pad of soft cotton cloth. Though this method is extensively used by professional furniture refinishers, that doesn't mean it is necessarily difficult to do.

Once you understand the procedure and have had a chance to practice first on an unimportant wood surface, you'll find many opportunities to use padding whenever a finishing defect occurs on any furniture in your home.

The most difficult part of padding is to find the right materials. You'll need to purchase "padding lacquer," which is so specialized that it is rarely sold in local paint and hardware stores. The easiest way of finding padding supplies is to order them directly from any of the large mail-order finishing supply firms (see Helpful Addresses for Ordering Supplies, page 60).

Padding is one of the quickest methods for repairing a finish because the padding lacquer actually dries as you massage it onto the wood. In addition, the squeegee action of the soft cotton pad used to spread the lacquer fills in minor cracks in the old finish at the same time. This time-saving feature is at least partially responsible for the popularity of the padding technique with professionals.

Prepare the padding cloth by rolling up a soft, clean piece of cotton so it is large enough to fit comfortably in your hand. Dip the pad into a bowl of padding lacquer and squeeze it out to remove any excess liquid.

Stroke the damaged wood surface with the moistened pad, using a small up-and-down rocking motion with your hand and wrist. This motion keeps the

Always keep padding cloth moving—solvents dry so quickly that a resting pad will leave cloth marks on wood

pad constantly moving at all times—an important consideration. Should the pad come to a full stop on the surface, the lacquer will quickly dry and the pad will stick to the wood, leaving an impression that resembles the weave of the cotton cloth.

Continue pouring lacquer onto the pad and moving it around the wood surface. Remember to quickly lift the pad off the surface when you have finished a particular area. Always start your padding motions gently just to wet the surface. Then gradually increase pressure to generate the heat that helps to dry the lacquer.

Rub the wood surface with the pad for at least 15 minutes to make sure all the lacquer is dry. The completed finish will usually be quite glossy. If you want a dull shine instead, rub the surface with 4/0 steel wool and apply a coat of paste wax.

PATCHING

Shellac-stick patching and wax-stick patching are useful techniques for repairing large scratches, gouges, and burns in the wood surface. Whenever you have a surface blemish that spoils an otherwise fine furniture finish, use one of these methods to camouflage the spot. Doing this will save yourself the trouble of a total refinishing job.

Shellac-stick patching is difficult to do without practice, but it's worthwhile to learn this useful procedure. Always practice the patching motions on a scrap of wood before attempting to repair a valuable piece of furniture.

Frequently you may not be able to find quality shellac sticks at your local paint or hardware store. In this case try purchasing them from any of the professional refinishers in your area or by mail order from any large wood finishing supply firm (see Helpful Addresses for Ordering Supplies, page 60).

You'll need other supplies, too. After you've gathered a small collection of colored shellac sticks you'll also require an alcohol lamp, a flexible artist's spatula (a common grapefruit knife also works well), a few sheets of 400-grit waterproof abrasive paper, and a small amount of paraffin rubbing oil.

Begin by choosing the shellac stick that most closely resembles the existing color of your wood. Heat the blade of the artist's spatula or knife and the tip of the shellac stick over the alcohol lamp.

Apply the molten shellac to the damaged wood surface, using the hot spatula to press the material smoothly into place. If the shellac cools too rapidly, reheat the spatula blade and stroke over the hardened shellac again.

When the damaged area has been repaired and the shellac has cooled, shave off any excess shellac with a sharp razor blade. Sand the repair with 400-grit waterproof abrasive paper lubricated with paraffin oil. Finally, touch up the spot with padding lacquer until it matches the surrounding surface sheen.

For shellac stick patching...

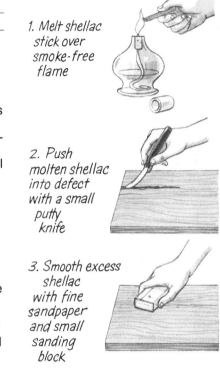

1. Melt shellac stick over smoke-free flame

2. Push molten shellac into defect with a small putty knife

3. Smooth excess shellac with fine sandpaper and small sanding block

Wax-stick patching is a much easier technique than shellac-stick patching, but wax is not nearly as durable or as permanent as shellac. Many wax stick colors are blended especially for retouching furniture and are available at all paint and hardware stores. However, ordinary wax crayons will also work well if necessary.

You will need basically the same equipment as that used for shellac-stick patching: a flexible artist's spatula or knife, an alcohol lamp, and a single-edge razor blade. A special refinisher's hot-patching iron can sometimes be substituted for the alcohol lamp. Look for the iron and instructions for its use in any large mail-order finishing supply catalog.

Choose your wax colors carefully to match the surrounding

undamaged wood surface. Occasionally you may have to blend two or more colors together to achieve a perfect match. Heat the wax and let it drip into the surface defect, completely filling the damaged area and leaving a slight excess of wax piled on top. Use a hot spatula blade or knife to force the wax deep into the blemish and to trim the repaired spot even with the surrounding surface.

Depending on your skill in applying wax with the spatula, a final touchup with the razor blade may or may not be necessary. If the repaired area is to receive any wear, prolong the life of the wax by covering it first with a coat of shellac and then with a coat of varnish or lacquer. An initial shellac coat is always necessary; without it, an additional finish won't adhere to the waxy repaired surface.

Specific defects and cures

Now that you're familiar with the five basic methods of rejuvenating a finish, decide which method is best for your particular finishing problem. Here is a list of the seven most common finish repair problems and suggested solutions.

White spots, rings, and blushing occur when water penetrates a shellac or lacquer finish. If moisture has penetrated completely through the finish into the wood, the white spots turn to black spots (see Dark Spots and Rings, this page) and the problem is much more severe.

A white, cloudy appearance is probably the most common finishing defect on furniture. Generally speaking, the whiter the area, the deeper the moisture has penetrated into the finish. However, many finishes can turn white just from the air's moisture.

Since white marks usually only occur in the finish itself, they are often quite easy to repair. Use the technique of abrasion to take care of minor problems, reamalgamation for major ones.

When only a slight trace of white is visible, vigorously rub a little toothpaste or moistened cigar ash into the wood surface with your finger. You'll find these common substances often contain all the abrasive action you need to remove the damage. Apply paste wax when the mark has disappeared.

Dents are slight depressions in the wood surface caused by falling objects or blows from blunt instruments. Dents occur more frequently in softwoods than in hardwoods, but in either case, repairs are basically the same.

To remove dents from unfinished furniture, place a wet cloth pad over the dent and hold a hot iron over the cloth; apply pressure. This steaming technique fills the wood fibers with water, causing them to swell. It may take anywhere from 15 minutes to 4 hours of steaming before the wood fibers resume their original shape.

To make the steaming process work for a dent on finished furniture, you'll have to remove the old finish, or puncture the existing finish with small pin holes. You could also resort to patching.

Scratches or hairline cracks on the finish that are not too severe can often be removed by reamalgamation. If a scratch has cut all the way into the wood, though, it will first have to be spot-stained to match the surrounding area before reamalgamation begins. When scratches are deep and much of the wood is missing, repair the area by patching. Repair polyurethanes (these can't be reamalgamated) by overcoating with another varnish.

Scars, gouges, and burns are often too conspicuous to be hidden by simple repairs. Whenever possible, try to remove all the old finish (see Removing the Old Finish, page 13) and completely refinish the wood.

If refinishing is out of the question, try to repair any large defect by patching. Before you patch a cigarette burn, though, be sure that you scrape all the burned wood away from the area with a sharp knife or razor blade.

Crazing is often caused by alternate expansion and contraction of wood under a finish, creating a pattern of very fine lines on a finished surface. This common problem (often termed "alligatoring") is usually taken care of quite easily by reamalgamation.

Worn and thin finishes often occur on furniture that receives intense daily use. Typically telltale signs of a worn-out finish are scuff marks and dull spots in areas of heaviest use, as well as minute surface scratches and places where the finish is worn completely through to the bare wood surface.

Repair a worn or thin old finish simply by overcoating with a new finish. If necessary, touch up the original surface color first by staining worn areas to match the surrounding wood.

Abused finishes include any that are so badly worn that they almost need total refinishing. Scratches in an abused finish are often deep enough to penetrate the surface of the wood, and the finish may be chipping off in a number of places.

Before completely refinishing the surface, try repairing it with padding. Although a lot of elbow grease will be needed to smooth out the old finish, the job usually isn't too difficult.

Dark spots and rings are some of the most serious damages that can happen to a furniture finish. These marks are caused by water that has penetrated through the surface finish and into the wood. On a good finish, damage like this doesn't happen in a few hours but usually has a longer-range cause —for example, a flower pot or something very moist that has been left on the wood for several days.

The only way to get rid of dark spots and rings is to remove the entire finish. Once you reach the bare wood surface, you can easily eliminate these marks with a solution of oxalic-acid crystals and water (see Oxalic Acid, page 26).

A guide to brushing & spraying

All finishing materials discussed in this book may be applied either by brushing or spraying them onto the furniture surface. (Though some furniture finishes can be poured directly onto the wood and wiped around with a rag, most home refinishers still rely on the traditional paintbrush.)

Brushing is the most common and initially one of the most economical methods of applying a finish, but it is much slower when compared to spray finishing. Spray guns and compressors are available in all shapes, sizes, and prices, and aerosol spray cans are popular for finishing small projects.

Whichever method you choose—brushing or spraying— make sure you are familiar with the principles involved before you begin your project.

BRUSHING IS THE TRADITIONAL WAY

The key to successful furniture finishing is to use good finishing tools. High-quality brushes are best for applying a finish smoothly and quickly and spreading it around evenly.

Why do good brushes help you to complete your work faster than bargain brushes do? For one thing, they carry more liquid in their long, well-shaped bristles so you won't have to dip them back in the finish quite as often. And high-quality brushes also lay on the finishing material so smoothly that you won't waste time repeatedly brushing back and forth for even coverage.

SELECTING A BRUSH

The best brush you can afford, properly cared for, is actually the most economical choice. Since it is simply impossible to do a good finishing job with a poor-quality brush, check the following points when you go brush shopping:

Bounce the brush bristles against the back of your hand. High-quality bristles will feel springy and elastic. Good bristles feel soft, silky, and resilient, and they spread evenly when you apply pressure. If bristles are too coarse, don't buy the brush—it won't spread the finish well.

Quality bristles spread smoothly, will feel springy to back of your hand

Flagged bristle tips (split & frayed) help spread finish evenly on the wood

Examine the bristle ends by spreading them between your fingers. All good brushes have bristles that are "flagged" (split and frayed) on the ends to produce the smoothest possible finish. The more "flags" on a bristle the better because flagging helps a bristle retain the finish and spread it smoothly onto the wood surface.

Hog and boar bristles have traditionally been the favorites of brush makers because these bristles are naturally flagged. Such natural bristles are not suitable for applying latex paints,

though, because the bristles soak up the water in the paints and quickly become soggy and useless.

Synthetic bristles, which are much more commonly available today, are artificially flagged and are best for applying water-base paints. Be careful when using a synthetic brush with strong chemical solvents, however. Some synthetic bristles may melt in finishes such as lacquer.

Check the ferrule or metal band that holds the bristles to the filler block and brush handle. All bristles should be solidly fastened to prevent any from falling out while the brush is in use. Fan the bristles with your hand to see if any loose bristles end up in your fingers. Loss of one or two bristles is normal, but any more than that and you'd be wise to choose a different brush.

Look at the filler block where the bristles hide beneath the ferrule. Many inexpensive brushes have a large filler block that leaves little room to include enough bristles. Good brushes have smaller filler blocks in which the bristles are set closer together.

Measure bristle length. High-quality brushes always have a blend of short and long bristles bound together in the ferrule. And long bristles should be long enough to flex easily. Always try to purchase a brush with bristles approximately 50 percent longer than the width of the brush.

PROPER BRUSHING TECHNIQUES

Successful brushing methods are often a mixture of common sense, good materials, and a little practical experience. Brushing is the most popular method of applying a finish because all brushes are relatively inexpensive when compared to the price of spray equipment, and using a brush is simple and straightforward. Hold the brush as you would a pencil with your fingers lightly gripping the metal ferrule. If you rest the handle between your thumb and first finger you'll find it easy to brush with long, steady strokes.

Never dip the brush bristles more than 1/3 to 1/2 their bristle length into the finish—more finish than that on the bristles will only work up into the ferrule and dry, making the brush difficult to clean.

When withdrawing the brush from the finish container, never drag the bristles over the container's edge to wipe off surplus finish. This practice will add air bubbles to the final finishing coat. Instead, "tip off" the ends of the bristles against the inside of the finish container before removing the brush. A good "tipping off" point is generally right above the level of the remaining finish.

Don't remove excess finish from brush on edge of can – air will be forced into bristles

Do squeeze off excess on inside of can above remaining liquid

Brush all large surface areas both with and against the grain to obtain the best finish coverage and to avoid skipping any areas. After you have covered the surface, finish all brush strokes, moving with the grain. Brush all table legs and other rounded shapes around the circumference with light, lengthwise strokes wherever possible. Use the edge or tip of the brush to work the finish well into furniture corners.

Each movement of your hand

should be smooth and even as you stroke the brush across the wood surface. If you apply excessive pressure to the brush bristles, you'll release too much finish. Always lift the brush gently from the surface at the end of each stroke to ensure an even coating.

Hints for successful brushing...

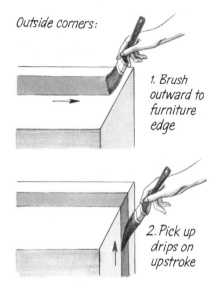

Outside corners:

1. Brush outward to furniture edge

2. Pick up drips on upstroke

Inside corners:

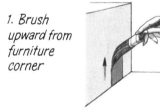

1. Brush upward from furniture corner

2. Pick up drips with outward stroke

Flat surfaces require that you brush all finishing materials out towards furniture edges. This brushing technique will prevent ugly drips that often result when a fully loaded finishing brush is pulled over a sharp edge. If you brush from lap mark to lap mark you'll be incorporating the excess finish from one stroke into the new finish of the following stroke. When painting or antiquing,

always continue brushing the surface until the finish is level and even. When applying shellac and polyurethane, though, allow these finishes to flow onto the wood and level out at their own rate. Whenever possible, avoid unnecessary brushing—it only makes finishing solvents evaporate more quickly, and your final results will suffer.

CLEANING A BRUSH

After you've used a good brush for the first time it will continue giving you a high-quality finish as it gets broken in, provided you take proper care of it. Always remember to clean your brush before the finishing material has had a chance to harden in the bristles.

When your finishing work is over for the day, soak your brush in a can of the correct solvent. Use paint thinner or turpentine to clean paint or varnish brushes, water for latex brushes, denatured alcohol for shellac brushes, and lacquer thinner for lacquer brushes.

After the brush bristles are thoroughly wet with solvent, remove any remaining finish by squeezing the bristles with your hand while holding the bristles skyward, letting the solvent wash the finish out of the ferrule. Repeat this process over and over again until a substantial amount of finish has been removed from the brush.

Empty the used solvent into another container for future reuse and pour new solvent into your cleaning can. Repeat the above cleaning process until no more finish can be squeezed from the bristles. Shake all the solvent out of the brush and straighten and smooth the bristles back to their original shape with a paintbrush comb available at all hardware and paint stores.

All manufacturers of quality brushes recommend that their brushes be cleaned thoroughly after each use. However, if you plan to continue the same finishing job the next day, you might want to experiment with ways of keeping your brush moist until then without cleaning it.

One such method involves suspending the brush in a container of the same solvent you would use for cleaning the brush.

With a hammer, pound a small nail into the wooden brush handle, right above the metal ferrule. Then hang the brush by the nail from the lip of a discarded coffee can filled with the proper solvent. Make certain that the bristles are completely submerged in the solvent, or else any leftover finish will dry in the ferrule. Be careful not to let your brush bristles rest on the bottom of the can; the flagged bristle tips will be ruined.

Another temporary storage method consists of wrapping your brush in a plastic bag and placing the whole thing in your refrigerator's freezer. Before you resume finishing the next day, let the brush have a chance to thaw; then work it around in a shallow can of solvent to loosen up the bristles.

STORING A BRUSH

When your finishing work is over and you plan on retiring your brush until the next finishing job comes along, take steps to store the brush correctly.

Begin by cleaning the brush thoroughly according to earlier instructions. When you feel that the brush is completely clean, try cleaning it at least once more just to be sure. Comb the bristles straight and then wrap the brush in heavy paper or aluminum foil to hold the bristles in place.

To store a brush...

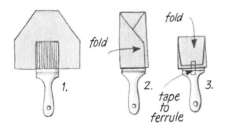

First clean; then wrap in heavy paper or aluminum foil for proper bristle protection

Hang the wrapped brush by the hole in the handle or store the brush flat in some out-of-the-way spot in your garage or workroom.

Brushes can also be stored by submerging them in solvent.

If you choose an old gallon can for your container, hang all your brushes from a piece of metal clothes hanger inserted through the holes in the brush handles and laid across the top opening of the can. If this type of container is to be used for a long period of time, though, you'll want to devise a cover for the can to reduce the rate of solvent evaporation.

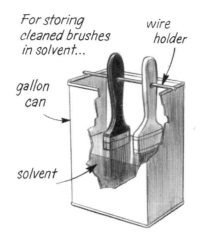

For storing cleaned brushes in solvent... wire holder gallon can solvent

SPRAY CAN FINISHING—PERFECT FOR SMALL PROJECTS

Aerosol spray cans are handy for applying a high-quality final covering to small furniture projects. Easy-to-use aerosols are available in a wide variety of finishes—shellac, polyurethane, lacquer, and enamel—and in a large choice of colors.

Though frequently more expensive than brush-on surface finishes, spray cans are ideally suited for such intricate finishing jobs as chairs, table legs, small novelty items, and wooden shutters. Spraying is also the best method of applying a finish over stencils, scorching, découpage, and decals.

CHOOSING YOUR AEROSOL FINISH

When choosing an aerosol finish, be sure to read the manufacturer's directions for application and the suggested hints before you begin to work. Since all aerosol finishes are highly flammable, never use a spray can near an open flame. Especially avoid spraying near the pilot light on a gas appliance.

Spray finishes also require special care in storage. Because the contents of these containers are under pressure and sensitive to temperature changes, don't store aerosols—even when empty—in places that are too sunny or warmer than 120° F. Puncturing and incinerating aerosols is another hazard because a sudden release of pressure in the containers can cause explosions and serious damage.

Each spray can is made up of four basic parts: the valve, the container, the propellant that produces the pressure, and the finishing material itself. To keep the finish in the container properly mixed, many spray cans contain a small ball that agitates the heavier finish particles at the bottom of the can when the can is shaken.

Unfortunately, many spray cans don't have sufficient power or a wide enough spray pattern to cover large surface areas. Another problem with spray cans is that they normally contain only highly thinned finishing materials that take longer to color and to build up a sufficiently protective finish. For major finishing projects, traditional brushing is a faster and often more efficient method of applying a finish.

TIPS FOR SUCCESS WITH SPRAY CANS

Even though an aerosol finish is under pressure, shaking the spray can is obviously an important preliminary finishing step. Without proper shaking the heavier finishing particles will remain at the bottom of the aerosol container, and the spray may come out too thin, or you may unknowingly use up all of the pressure in the can before you use up all the finish.

Before you begin to work, remember that one of the biggest problems in spray finishing is overspray. A fine aerosol spray is usually quite difficult to confine to the specific project you're working on; it always seems to drift through the air and settle on surrounding surfaces instead.

To avoid this overspray, take special precautions to screen off your work area and to protect all nearby surfaces. If you must do your spraying inside, use old bed sheets, newspapers, or plastic dropcloths to cover vulnerable surfaces. Whenever possible, though, do all your spraying outdoors or in the garage rather than in the house.

It's important to hold the nozzle the proper distance from the surface when applying an aerosol finish. At least 10 to 12 inches away from the surface is recommended. Always keep the spray nozzle parallel with the surface; be sure to press the button down as far as it will go.

For choosing proper spray can distance...

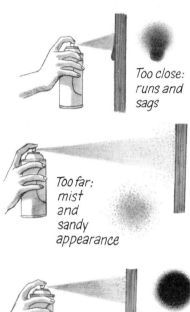

Too close: runs and sags

Too far: mist and sandy appearance

Correct distance: uniform controlled coverage

10 to 12 inches

If the nozzle is held closer to the surface, too much paint will be applied, causing runs or sags in the finish. If the nozzle is held too far away, particles of paint will begin to dry before reaching the surface and the resulting finish will be poor.

Always keep your spray strokes moving evenly from side to side or from top to bottom of the surface you're finishing. Spray the corners of your furniture first, with the spray pattern overlapping in the center of the corner and extending slightly outward. Try to work from a finished area into an unfinished area so that any overspray won't mar a previously finished surface.

Direct the spray onto the surface by moving the can with your entire arm. If the can is moved only in small arcs instead

of in long, parallel strokes, the resulting finish will be poorly distributed. You'll find that the finish is too heavy in the center of the stroke and too thin at each end.

Recommended spray can movement

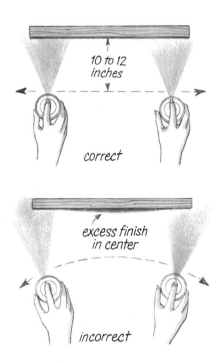

10 to 12 inches

correct

excess finish in center

incorrect

Be sure that each new stroke overlaps 1/3 to 1/2 of the preceding stroke. This will insure an even finishing coat without streaks. Never end a stroke in the middle of your project because too much finish may build up and runs or sags may develop.

After each use of your spray can invert the container and press the nozzle until you're sure it is free of finish. Any finish remaining in the nozzle after use will only dry, clogging the nozzle and preventing it from being used again.

After using spray can, clean nozzle by inverting can and pressing button for a short blast of pure propellant

SPRAY GUN FINISHING SAVES TIME

By far the fastest method of applying a wood finish is with a spray gun. Spray guns and compressors are extremely useful to the house painter and the furniture finisher because they are relatively simple to operate.

In addition, their versatility often helps them pay for themselves in a short period of time. Once you've completed your spray finishing, you can use any remaining extra air to inflate your auto tires, bike tires, or for many other purposes.

While sometimes fairly expensive, several varieties of modern spray guns and air compressors are now within the financial reach of nearly everyone. Airless or electric sprayers are also available. Though some of these are inexpensive when compared to the more complicated air pressure models, their output is not significantly greater than that of an ordinary spray can.

If you choose not to purchase your own spray equipment, you can usually rent a spray gun or compressor at a hardware store or retail rental shop.

A typical pressurized spray system often consists of a spray gun that holds and distributes the finishing material, an air compressor (either gasoline-powered or electric) that provides the propellant for the gun, and sometimes a holding tank to equalize and store the air pressure until needed. Airless or electric spray systems are self-contained and have a small, high-speed pump driven by an electric vibrator already built into the spray gun's handle.

TYPES OF SPRAY GUNS

Quality spray guns are basically one of two types—siphon feed or pressure feed. Each type has its own advantages and disadvantages, depending on the type of finish you choose. Combination guns are available.

Siphon feed spray guns use a blast of pure air from the gun's nozzle to create a vacuum in the open tubes that lead directly to the finishing material. This vacuum pulls the finish up and out of the container where it is mixed with the air and then sprayed onto the wood surface. Since the air and paint combine outside the spray gun, this is called an "external mix" gun construction.

A siphon feed gun is most popular with wood finishers who primarily use spray lacquer and other light-bodied finishes. Lacquer is such a fast-drying material that use of a siphon feed gun prevents the finish from drying inside and around the nozzle opening. Siphon feed guns are easy to clean and can be used to spray finishes from a wide variety of glass jars or other open containers.

Types of spray gun nozzles...

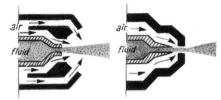

*External mix –
siphon feed*

*Internal mix –
pressure feed*

Pressure feed spray guns use a small portion of air pressure to force the finishing material up from the pressurized container and out through the gun's nozzle. Since the finish in this gun is under pressure, it is possible to use a pressure feed gun to spray such thicker finishing materials as enamels and polyurethanes.

On a pressure feed spray gun, the air and finish can be mixed both outside the nozzle (external mix) and inside the nozzle (internal mix), depending on the type of finish you will be using. External mix guns are most useful for spraying latex-type paints; internal mix spray guns are best for spraying paints with an oil base. Most spray guns you can purchase today can be adjusted to spray either way.

A pressure feed gun is probably the best all-around spray gun for the furniture finisher to purchase. It's far more useful than a siphon feed gun because it sprays any weight of finishing material that can also be applied by a brush. However, a pressure feed gun can only be cleaned or used when the finish or solvent is enclosed in the correct pressurized metal cup that comes with the gun.

THE AIR COMPRESSOR

Modern air-compressing units are commonly either piston or diaphragm types. The piston compressor uses a motor to drive a piston in a cylinder, much like the piston action in an automobile engine. When the piston moves down to the bottom of the cylinder, air is sucked in; when the piston moves up, air is compressed and pushed out of the cylinder.

Though very similar to the piston compressor, the diaphragm compressor uses a rubber diaphragm instead of the metal piston. This diaphragm compressor operates without oil and is lighter in weight and less expensive than a piston unit.

All air compressors are run by motors, the horsepower of the motor determining the size and capacity of the whole spray finishing unit. A unit with a motor of from 1/4 to 1/3 horsepower is about the smallest that can be used for satisfactory spray finishing. Larger 1 horsepower units can easily apply 6 cubic feet of liquid per minute at 40 psi (pounds per square inch)—more than adequate for any finishing job.

THE SPRAY BOOTH

If you do more and more spray finishing, you may want to consider developing a spray booth. The ideal spray booth for the furniture finishing perfectionist often consists of a separate room that blocks out the dust of the workshop and is equipped with a turntable, a paint storage cabinet, and an exhaust fan with an explosion-proof motor.

Since a 5 by 5 foot area will be large enough to handle most finishing projects, a novice furniture finisher can set up a spray booth nearly anywhere. In a pinch, a shower curtain can be hung in a spare corner of the workshop or garage. The curtain will prevent the finishing overspray from spreading beyond a limited area; it will also keep dust and dirt off the newly sprayed project.

A turntable is an important piece of spray booth equipment highly useful for spraying furniture. Often homemade, turntables can closely resemble the "Lazy Susans" frequently found on many large dining room tables.

For wood finishing, the turntable rotates the project in front of the finisher so the entire project receives an even, overall spray.

Build your own spray turntable...

use scrap lumber, four swivel casters, a pipe flange, and a pipe center post; fit center post into a hole in a firm base so it can revolve

Since high-quality exhaust fans are expensive, many uninformed beginning finishers try to get along without this vital accessory. But because spray finishes release toxic fumes into the air, there must always be some way of eliminating fumes from the work area. If an exhaust fan is definitely out of the question, always be careful to spray furniture with at least two windows open to provide adequate cross ventilation.

OPERATING A SPRAY GUN

Techniques for using a spray gun are similar to those used for spray can finishing. But spray guns are far more complicated than aerosols because they must be properly adjusted before spraying begins. Always be certain to read any manufacturer's directions supplied with the gun, air compressor, or specific finish you're using.

If spray gun finishing is new to you, practice various spraying techniques on one or two old cardboard boxes before you actually begin to apply finish to your furniture. Experiment with the full range of fluid and pressure adjustments available on your spray gun. A few minutes of practicing with the spray gun and air compressor will give you the proper "feel" of spray finishing, along with enough know-how to tackle an actual project.

Begin to spray by moving the gun in long strokes parallel to the work surface and pivoting from your shoulder. If you move the spray gun only with your wrist, you'll "arc" each stroke, ending up with too much finish in the center of the stroke and too little finish on either end. At the beginning and end of each stroke, the spray gun should be triggered to avoid buildup on the ends of the sprayed surface. The speed of each stroke should be about the same as if you were using a brush.

Always try to keep the spray gun between 8 to 10 inches away from the surface you're spraying. The closer the gun is to the surface, the higher the concentration of finish that will be sprayed. Spraying close to the surface must be done *rapidly* to prevent runs and sags in the finish. When the gun is held too far from the surface, each stroke must be *slowed down* or the finishing material will not have a chance to collect. For professional spraying results, move the gun in straight, uniform strokes back and forth across the wood surface. Each new spray pattern should overlap 1/3 to 1/2 of the last spray pattern. By aiming each new stroke at the bottom of the preceding stroke, you'll always get solid spray coverage without streaks, runs, or dry spots.

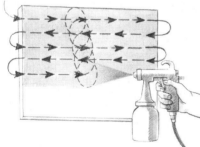

For even coverage with spray gun, spray from side to side, slightly overlapping each preceding stroke

When you spray level surfaces, always begin spraying on the side of the piece closest to you and work toward its far side. This technique is especially important in lacquer spraying because any lacquer overspray that lands on previously sprayed work will dry to a sandy texture. Since paint and synthetic finishing are also susceptible to overspray, plan your spray sequence ahead of time to avoid any such problems.

When spraying flat surfaces, you'll often have to tilt the spray gun slightly; an angle of about 45° down toward the surface with the spray cup at least half full is recommended. Whenever the piece itself can be tilted or laid on one side instead, do so to minimize the need to tilt the spray gun.

SPRAYING FURNITURE

Proper spraying of furniture requires a certain routine to complete the job with the least amount of time, effort, and overspray. Always adjust for a small spray pattern on the spray gun nozzle to permit close control of the finish.

If you don't want to spray certain parts of your furniture, cover them with newspaper and masking tape before you begin. If you direct the force of the spray away from the taped edge, the result will be an even, fine line where the finish has stopped. Always remove masking tape soon after you finish spraying because it has a tendency to harden if it remains on the surface.

Finish all flat furniture surfaces, such as table tops and dresser sides, by applying a band of spray to furniture's edges first and then spraying the center of the surface with long, back and forth strokes.

Spray all corners first, with spray pattern overlapping both sides of corner evenly

correct   incorrect

When finishing a table, begin by spraying all legs on their inner sides and then on their outer sides; then spray around the outer edges of the table and end by spraying the table top. These

steps could easily be reversed, of course, but the important thing is to decide on a specific finishing order before beginning work to minimize overspray on finished areas. If you always spray furniture following these guidelines, you'll get better results with a minimum of problems.

Typical spraying sequence for a kitchen table

1: *Inside surfaces of legs*
2: *Outside surfaces of legs*
3: *Outer sides of table*
4: *Table top*

CLEANING A SPRAY GUN

Proper cleaning is always necessary for trouble-free spray gun performance. Never under any circumstances let the finishing material you've used have a chance to dry and harden inside your spray gun.

When you've completed spraying, fill the spray cup 1/2 full with the correct solvent for the finish you were using. Use water to clean latex paints, paint thinner or turpentine for oil paints or polyurethane varnishes, alcohol for shellac, and lacquer thinner for lacquer. If the spray gun is of the siphon feed variety, the solvent can be poured into any open container. A pressure feed gun, though, requires solvent supplied in the proper pressurized cup.

Now all you need is an out-of-the-way place where you can spray the solvent out of the gun as you would a regular finish. The solvent will clean every area where the finish has been, leaving the gun ready for the next time it is needed.

Step-by-step finishing guide

Included in this section are step-by-step instructions for applying the 10 most popular furniture finishes. Many of the instructions include specific page numbers so that you can refer back to earlier chapters if necessary for more detailed information on individual procedures.

First choose the wood finish you want to use (see Choosing a Final Finish, page 35); then follow the suggested finishing schedule given here.

PENETRATING RESIN FINISH —DANISH OIL

Easy to apply and maintain, this durable finish lets you enjoy the natural texture and "feel" of the wood grain.

1) Properly prepare the wood surface as you would for any furniture finish (see Preparing the Wood Surface, page 20). When the surface is completely smooth, go over it once more to ensure open wood pores that will allow for even resin penetration.

2) Stain the furniture if you desire a surface color. Use only lightly pigmented or water-base stains to leave room in the wood pores for the resin finish to absorb (see What Staining Can Do, page 29).

3) Pour on a liberal amount of the resin, wiping it around on the surface with a small pad of 3/0 steel wool. Keep the entire surface wet for at least 15 minutes to allow the resin to penetrate thoroughly, adding more resin if necessary (see Easy-To-Use Synthetics, page 36).

4) When surface penetration stops, wipe the wood dry with a soft, absorbent cloth.

5) If a second coat of resin is necessary, apply it 3 to 4 hours after the first coat.

6) For greater surface luster, let the finish dry for at least 4 hours; then briskly rub the surface with a small piece of 4/0 steel wool,

using a little of the resin for lubrication.

7) When the wood has absorbed all the penetrating finish it can, dry the surface thoroughly with a clean cloth; then polish rapidly with another cloth.

8) If an even higher surface luster is desired, apply 2 or more coats of a good paste wax (see Rubbing & Waxing, pages 48-49) after the resin has dried.

CATALYTIC SEALER FINISH

Use this finish to obtain the "wood-under-glass" look of clear liquid plastic.

1) Sand the wood thoroughly and remove all surface imperfections (see Smoothing the Wood, page 20).

For smoother sanding, lightly wet back of sandpaper to increase flexibility

2) Stain the furniture if a surface color is desired, but avoid using heavily pigmented stains whenever possible. The catalytic adhesion is often poor over anything but a bare wood surface.

3) Mix the synthetic resin with the required amount of catalyst, following the manufacturer's directions. Always use new solutions within 1 hour of mixing before they harden.

4) Apply the catalytic solution evenly to the wood surface with either brush or spray (see Easy-to-Use Synthetics, page 36). Use a strip of masking tape around the edges of the surface if you want a thick, no-drip finish.

5) When the surface is dry (usually in 1 to 2 hours), sand with extra-fine (320 to 400-grit) abrasive paper.

6) Apply a second coat of the catalytic solution if necessary. Dry overnight.

7) Rub and polish the surface for a high shine if desired (see Rubbing & Waxing, pages 48-49).

Caution: Some catalytic finishes require baking under medium-high heat (see Catalytic Sealers, page 37).

BASIC OIL FINISH

Natural and synthetic oil finishes penetrate the wood pores to give a traditional look and feel to furniture surfaces.

1) Make sure the wood surface is clean and bare of all old finish, sanding dust, oily fingerprints, or dirt.

2) Since boiled linseed oil often colors the wood quite nicely, there is usually no need to apply any additional stain.

3) You can use pure boiled linseed oil by itself as a finish, but it's always a good idea to mix it with an equal amount of gum turpentine to ensure adequate drying.

4) Pour or wipe boiled linseed oil onto the wood and spread it generously over the entire surface with a rag (see Oil for a Natural Finish, page 37).

5) After the oil has had time to adequately soak into the wood pores, rub the surface rapidly with a clean, thick cloth to bring out the luster of the finish.

6) Use anywhere from 4 to 40 coats of oil and always be sure to repeat the rubbing process between each coat. Never apply more oil until the previous coat of oil has dried throughly.

7) To keep the surface looking like new, repeat the oil rub annually for the life of your furniture.

Caution: When applying oil to wood, always apply it to the inside and underside of a surface as well as to the outside and top of the piece. Only by spreading an even coat of oil on *all* exposed wood can you prevent the wood from warping.

BASIC SHELLAC FINISH

A shellac finish lies on the wood surface, providing an attractive and durable shield of protection against scratches and dropped objects.

1) Sand or rub the wood surface with steel wool until it is perfectly smooth—the smoother the surface, the better the final finish (see Preparing the Wood Surface, page 20).

2) If you want to change the wood's color, apply any popular wood stain and let it dry thoroughly before further finishing (see Coloring the Wood, page 29). If you use a water stain, be sure to rub the surface with fine steel wool after the stain has dried because water always tends to raise wood grain.

3) When the stain is dry, apply a wash coat of very thin shellac mixed 1 part shellac to 4 parts denatured alcohol (see Sealing the Surface, page 27). After this sealer coat dries, rub it with 4/0 steel wool to smooth the surface.

4) Apply two more coats of shellac in the same manner. For easy brushing, thin 1 part shellac with 1 or 2 parts denatured alcohol. Let each coat dry thoroughly before applying the next coat (see The Classic Look of Shellac, page 38), and be sure to scuff-sand with 4/0 steel wool between coats for the smoothest possible finish.

ADVANCED SHELLAC FINISH

For the classic shellac look, a little extra effort might be worth your while.

1) Carefully prepare the wood surface by sanding, bleaching, and repairing any blemishes that might show through the final finish.

2) Stain the wood if color is desired. Any quality stain will work (see Coloring the Wood, page 29), but be sure to let the stain dry thoroughly before applying the finish. Use paste wood filler if nec-

essary on open-grained woods.

3) Apply a thin coat of shellac (1-pound cut) to act as a sealer and to provide a base for subsequent finishing coats (see Sealing the Surface, page 27). Let the surface dry for at least 1 hour and scuff-sand with extra-fine 220 to 320-grit abrasive paper or with 4/0 steel wool.

4) Apply from two to four additional coats of shellac in the same way. Allow each coat to dry at least one hour longer than the previous coat. Be sure to continue scuff-sanding between coats.

To avoid drips, build a masking tape dam around edge of a table top before finishing

5) When the final coat has dried at least 6 hours, rub the newly shellacked surface smooth with 400 or 600-grit waterproof abrasive paper wrapped around a good sanding block (see Rubbing & Waxing, page 49). Lubricate the waterproof paper with paraffin oil—never use water on shellac.

6) After the surface is glassy smooth to the touch, place a small amount of paste wax on a soft cloth and apply the wax evenly to the wood.

7) After the wax has dried for 10 to 20 minutes, begin rubbing the surface briskly in a circular motion with a clean, soft cloth to buff the wax. Let the surface dry for 1 hour or more. Repeat waxing and buffing as necessary.

BASIC POLYURETHANE VARNISH FINISH

These long-lasting synthetic varnishes are easily applied and give the surface a hard, clear finish im-

pervious to moisture, alcohol, chemicals, and burns.

1) Sand the surface until it's as smooth as you can make it. Any irregularities or blemishes left on the wood at this stage will only be emphasized by the clear final finish.

2) Stain the wood for a more attractive color or tone (see Coloring the Wood, page 29). Whenever possible, use a stain that is guaranteed to be compatible with the final polyurethane finish you've chosen; check the manufacturer's label to be sure. Let the stain dry thoroughly before further finishing.

3) Apply one to three liberal coats of a good satin or gloss polyurethane. Try not to let more than 24 hours elapse between coats; otherwise poor adhesion may result. Scuff the wood surface between coats with 220-grit abrasive paper or 3/0 steel wool for a smoother final finish.

ADVANCED POLYURETHANE VARNISH FINISH

This glossy surface will bring out the rich texture and grain of the wood. If you like, apply a coat of satin polyurethane for the hand-rubbed look.

1) Prepare the wood surface by carefully sanding, bleaching, and repairing any surface blemishes that might detract from the clear final finish. Make sure the wood is clean and free of all sanding dust, oily fingerprints, or traces of old finish. Use a sanding sealer that you're sure is compatible with urethane resins for an extra-smooth surface (see Sealing the Surface, page 27).

2) Change the wood color by staining, if you like. Practically any high-quality stain will work well as long as you allow ample drying time before further finishing. Always read the manufacturer's label on your polyurethane finish to see if one stain is recommended over another.

3) On open-grain woods—such as mahogany, oak, and walnut—if you use a filler, be sure to choose one that is compatible with polyurethane (see To Fill or Not to Fill, page 32). Be sure to let the filler dry thoroughly before continuing.

4) When the filler is dry, apply

one to three coats of gloss poly-urethane to bring out the rich texture and grain of the wood surface. Scuff lightly with 220-grit abrasive paper between coats.

5) If you would rather not leave the surface glossy, use 320-grit waterproof abrasive paper or 4/0 steel wool and oil to rub the finish down to a dull glow. Or, if you prefer, you might consider applying a coat of satin polyurethane over the last gloss application. This will give you nearly the same hand-rubbed look and add an extra coat of surface protection at the same time.

Caution: Omit the paste filler stage if you intend to apply several coats of polyurethane because the polyurethane will act as its own filler.

BASIC LACQUER FINISH

Harder and more versatile than shellac, lacquer is usually applied with a spray gun or aerosol can. If you plan to use a brush, be sure to purchase brushing lacquer.

1) Sand the surface thoroughly to remove all surface defects and to make the wood grain level (see Preparing the Wood Surface, page 20).

2) Sponge the surface with warm water to raise the wood grain slightly. Allow the surface to dry at least 1 hour before continuing.

3) When the surface has dried, sand the wood again with 220-grit fine abrasive paper and dust the surface thoroughly.

4) If staining is necessary, use only a water stain or a non-grain-raising stain (choose the long-drying type so it will be easy to apply with a brush). Oil stain is not used with lacquer unless you first apply a lacquer sanding sealer because the stain will often bleed through succeeding lacquer coats. Let the surface dry overnight.

5) Apply one coat of clear gloss lacquer and be sure you purchase brushing lacquer if you use a brush (see Lacquer: Fast, Dust-Free Drying, page 45). When the surface is dry, scuff with 320-grit abrasive paper.

6) Apply a final coat of lacquer, using either gloss or flat finish, depending on the surface sheen you want.

ADVANCED LACQUER FINISH

Quick-drying lacquer finishes are applied most successfully with spray equipment. For professional results, always practice your spraying techniques before you begin.

1) First prepare the wood by thoroughly sanding, bleaching, and repairing any blemishes or irregularities on the surface.

Spot-stain all repairs to match surrounding wood

2) Sponge the wood surface quickly with warm water and allow it to dry at least 1 hour before continuing.

3) Lightly sand the wood once more with 220-grit fine abrasive paper. Be sure to remove all sanding dust from the surface before further finishing.

4) Stain the wood if necessary with a good NGR stain (see What Staining Can Do, page 29). Spray the stain on and allow it to dry 12 hours before continuing. Do not use an oil stain unless you're experienced with advanced lacquer techniques—the stain will bleed through the following finish coats.

5) Spray a thin coat of lacquer sanding sealer over the stain to seal it (see Sealing the Surface, page 27). Then sand lightly with 320-grit abrasive paper, being careful not to sand through the stain.

6) If the wood is open-grain mahogany, oak, or walnut, apply paste wood filler for a perfectly smooth surface (see To Fill or Not to Fill, page 32). When the filler has dried for at least 48 hours, lightly sand with 320-grit abrasive paper.

7) Spray another thin coat of lacquer sanding sealer over the filler as you did over the stain. When the surface is dry, sand lightly with 320 to 400-grit abrasive paper and remove any trace of sanding dust.

8) After a day or two, when you're sure every finishing coat you've applied is completely dry, apply another two or more coats of a gloss lacquer with spray equipment. Make sure each coat has an adequate time to dry before applying the next coat. If imperfections occur, let the finish dry for at least 2 hours. Then lightly sand those areas with 320-grit abrasive paper.

9) If you want the appearance of a rubbed finish rather than that of a glossy shine, apply a final coat of semigloss or flat lacquer. Or, if you like, rub the last gloss coat with pumice and rubbing oil (see Rubbing & Waxing, pages 48-49) to dull the sheen.

10) Finish your surface with a good application of paste wax, rubbing briskly around in a circular motion; then buff the wax with a soft, clean cloth.

STANDARD ENAMEL FINISH

Versatile and easy to apply, opaque enamel finishes can be used in situations where a clear wood finish is not practical.

1) Surface preparation is one of the most important steps in this finish. If you've used a previous finish for the base coat, make sure it is still adhering well to the bare wood. Sand all old finishes thoroughly with 180 to 220-grit abrasive paper to prepare for the new coat of enamel. If you plan on enameling new furniture, carefully sand it so all surface blemishes and construction marks are removed.

2) If the wood surface already has a finish, it will serve as an excellent undercoat. If the surface is bare wood, though, brush on any enamel undercoat that is compatible with your final finish (see Color & Cover with Enamel, page 46). If you like, you can tint the undercoat to match the final surface color.

3) When the undercoat has dried, sand the wood lightly with 220 to 280-grit abrasive paper. Remove all sanding dust from the surface.

4) Brush or spray the first enamel coat on the wood. When dry, scuff sand with 280 to 320-grit waterproof abrasive paper.

5) Apply a second coat of enamel if necessary for color and added surface protection.

A glossary of terms

Antique. Any piece of furniture from an older style or period. Traditionally, that which is more than 100 years old.

Base coat. The first coat upon which additional coats are applied. The basic color coat used under a toner or glaze for an antique finish.

Bleeding. A problem occurring with some stains and fillers when their solids, dissolved by the solvents of certain finishes, become part of those finishes.

Boiled linseed oil. Refers to raw linseed oil that has been heated and cooled to improve its drying ability. Currently, most linseed oils are "boiled" by adding chemical driers instead of by heating.

Catalytic finishes. These are usually two-part finishes, resin and hardener, often supplied in separate containers in liquid or powder form.

Crazing. A fine, netlike pattern of fine cracks often found on aged finishes. Also called alligatoring.

Cut. The number of pounds of shellac resin dissolved in a gallon of solvent. Four lbs. of dry shellac flakes dissolved in 1 gal. denatured alcohol makes a 4 lb. cut.

Découpage. The craft of mounting pictures or designs on wooden or metal surfaces, followed by multiple coats of a clear finish.

Denatured alcohol. The proven solvent for shellac.

Distressing. Selectively damaging wood or its finish so that it appears to be aged or worn.

Epoxy. A durable synthetic resin noted for its tremendous adhesive powers. Often found in many modern finishes and glues.

Filler. Wood filler is used to fill the pores of such open-pored woods as oak or walnut in order to provide a flat, smooth surface for finishing.

Flat. A finish texture that produces absolutely no reflections.

Gesso. A mixture of plaster of Paris, water, and water-soluble white glue used to create raised designs and to provide a smooth, porous surface for a final finish.

Glossy. A finish texture that is silky smooth, with a highly reflective (but not mirrorlike) finish.

Grain. The pattern produced in a wood surface by the fiber structure of the wood.

Hardwood. A term designating wood from non-coniferous (noncone-bearing) trees. Not a literal term, since many so-called hardwoods are actually softer than those called softwoods.

Kerf. The path cut through wood by a saw blade.

Knot. The result of branching or budding in a tree. Usually a darker colored mark in wood where the grain is at right angles to the normal grain pattern.

Latex. A name commonly applied to any water-base varnish or enamel.

Lubricant. Any material used between two rubbing surfaces to reduce friction or, in the case of sanding, to reduce clogging in the abrasive grit.

Mineral spirits. A less expensive thinner and solvent than turpentine, frequently used in paints and varnishes.

N.G.R. stain. Nongrain-raising stains, made with fast-drying solvents that do not swell or raise wood grain.

Opaque. In finishing terms, any finish that obscures the wood surface. Literally, impervious to light.

Overcoating. Completely coating a surface or previous finish with a new finish.

Padding. Using a pad or wad of material to apply a finish to a wood surface with only a wiping motion of the wrist.

Patina. A special surface coloration that develops in woods over a period of time.

Pigment. Fine powder used to provide color and camouflage to stains and final finishes.

Polyurethane. One variety of urethane resin used in varnish and enamel manufacturing.

Pores. Small voids or pits in wood surfaces that are actually the open ends of the tree's sap vessels.

Pumice. A volcanic rock that, in powder form, is used as a fine abrasive for reducing the gloss of a shiny finish.

Reamalgamation. The process of applying solvent to an already hardened finish to soften that finish. The solvent then evaporates, leaving the finish in like-new condition.

Resins. Natural or synthetic materials, usually transparent or translucent, that are soluble in organic solvents (but not water). Used in producing woodworking and metalworking finishes.

Rottenstone. A finely ground silica containing limestone used for very fine abrasive polishing. Also called tripoli.

Sanding sealer. A very thin finishing wash coat designed to seal wood surfaces and even out irregular hardness for smoother sanding.

Sap. The life fluid of a tree, the residue of which is encountered in finishing as a gummy pitch around knots and streaks, especially in fir and pine.

Sap streak. Pockets or cracks containing pitch deposits that will interfere with adhesion or finish hardening unless shielded by shellac.

Satin. A finish texture having a soft sheen similar to that of satin or silk material.

Saturated solution. A solution in which the liquid can dissolve no more of the material being added.

Scuff. The process of roughening a too-smooth surface just enough to encourage good adhesion for the following coat. Especially used when applying varnishes.

Sealer. A liquid finishing material designed to seal or shield the surface from excessive penetration by other finishing materials.

Solvent. Any liquid that will dissolve a material.

Stick shellac. Dry shellac resin in stick form with selected color additives. Closely approximates standard wood and stain colors. Most often used as a hot-melt patching material on wood surfaces.

Syringe. Used for applying thin glue behind loose joints when you can't disassemble the furniture.

Tack rag. A tacky, varnish-soaked piece of cheesecloth, or other lint-free material, used to wipe surfaces free of dust before finishing.

Tacky. That point at which a sticky surface grabs or pulls at anything touching it but is not readily removed from the original surface.

Thinner. Any volatile liquid compatible with a liquid finish and used to reduce its consistency.

Top coat. One coat of finish which covers another. Usually applied as the final coat.

Undercoat. Any finishing material first coat used under a final or top coat.

Veneer. A thin surface layer of wood or other material used to add durability or beauty to an otherwise unsuitable surface.

Index